Heart and Spirit
REBORN

Heart and Spirit
REBORN

A Fan's Journal of the 2010-2011
Toronto Maple Leafs

DOUG MAGWOOD

Order this book online at www.trafford.com
or email orders@trafford.com

Most Trafford titles are also available at major online book retailers.

Printed in the United States of America.

ISBN: 978-1-4269-7894-4 (sc)
ISBN: 978-1-4269-7895-1 (e)

Library of Congress Control Number: 2011912830

Trafford rev. 07/22/2011

 www.trafford.com

North America & International
toll-free: 1 888 232 4444 (USA & Canada)
phone: 250 383 6864 ♦ fax: 812 355 4082

Foreword

Bryan Lewis

Being a former National Hockey League Official and subsequent Director of Officiating of the NHL, I was able to witness and appreciate the fervour and passion of hockey fans from coast to coast in both Canada and the United States of America.

As an on-ice official, I worked more than 1000 regular season games in every NHL city, even some, such as Cleveland, Kansas City and Oakland, that no longer house franchises. I also officiated in 89 playoff games, and four assignments in the Stanley Cup Finals. This alone does not make me a hockey expert, but it does allow me to recognize those with dedication, passion and loyalty to particular teams and players.

Throughout my hockey career, I have lived in a small town northwest of Toronto, Ontario now known as Halton Hills. It is a town created by the amalgamation of Georgetown, Acton, and the rural area between. Our town has become known as a hockey hotbed, with a fan base loyal to both local and NHL teams. The central debate has, for the most part, been the long-time rivalry between Montreal and Toronto. For example, our current mayor Rick Bonnette is a sincere Canadien fan, while his wife, Josey, is a staunch supporter of the Maple Leafs. In recent years we see fans of Vancouver, Calgary, Edmonton, and now Winnipeg sporting their teams' jerseys on the streets and in the arenas of Georgetown and Acton.

Among the citizens of our town lives a gentleman named Doug Magwood. Doug is a former teacher, Vice-Principal and Principal who served his entire teaching career in Halton. As an educator, he coached in several school sporting activities including volleyball, basketball, softball, and track & field. He also served his community as a volunteer ambulance attendant, Library Board trustee, and completed two full terms as a board member with Crime Stoppers of Halton.

I believe that Doug is one of the most loyal Toronto Maple Leaf fans in Ontario. In the 1950's, Doug jumped on the Maple Leaf bandwagon, and stayed on it. He has survived uninjured over the years, unlike hundreds of others who chose to jump on and off that bandwagon as the team's fortunes rose and fell. He has been a faithful rider for nearly six decades.

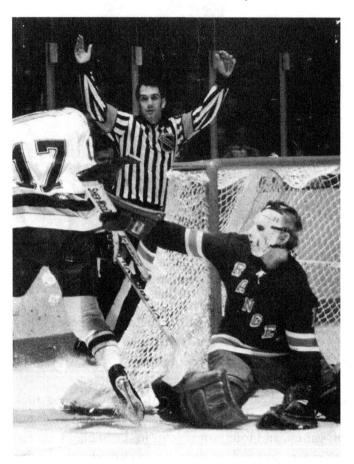

Referee Bryan Lewis Stops the Play

I am pleased to contribute the Foreword for Doug's current book about the Leafs. Nine years ago, he wrote and published his first such book, entitled **<u>Heart and Spirit: A Fan's Journal of the Toronto Maple Leafs of 2001 – 2002</u>.** In this newest volume, entitled **<u>Heart & Spirit Reborn</u>**, I can simply state that you will read about the rigors of a long and hard-fought Maple Leaf season in the NHL. You will also be privy to bold commentary regarding players, coaches and yes, even NHL Management. Doug does not hold back in his praise and candid assessment of all in the Leaf organization OR the NHL Head Office.

You will read a very accurate account of the most recent season played by the Toronto Maple Leafs through the eyes of a passionate fan of the blue and white.

In addition to his hockey writing, Doug has also collaborated with his friend Jack Reed, to produce a book entitled **A New Preaching Place in Georgetown,** (1998), which related the history of St. Andrew's United Church in the community of Georgetown. Doug and Jack added to their original work upon the church's fiftieth anniversary in 2008.

Doug has been a haemodialysis patient for more than ten years at Credit Valley Hospital in Mississauga, Ontario. His long struggle with kidney disease has never diminished his passion for Maple Leaf hockey. **As a gesture of his appreciation for the many years of care by the nurses, doctors and support staff of CVH, Doug is donating all proceeds from the sale of his book to the Renal Department at Credit Valley.**

The Toronto Maple Leaf logo is very close to Doug's heart. Enjoy the read, share the passion, and continue to wait with Doug, and the rest of us for the Stanley Cup Parade Route in Toronto to be announced. After 44 years, who knows, that date might be right around the corner.

Bryan Lewis,

Former NHL Official & Director of Officiating
Present Councillor - Town of Halton Hills
OUA Referee in Chief

July, 2011

Acknowledgements

Writing a book of any kind takes a great deal of effort. Having undertaken a project like this on several occasions over the past decade, I can readily attest to that as a statement of fact. As the author of this volume, I spend approximately one hour per page in order to present my best work before my readers. There is, of course, a first draft. Then comes the spelling and punctuation check. Following that, I re-read my initial work to make sure that there is minimal repetition of words or phrases. Frequently, more thoughts occur to me, or additional information needs to be provided, therefore additional revision is required. When I think my work is complete, I read it one more time before saving and printing the final copy.

An author cannot complete a book alone. The end product is the result of input from several sources. I wish to acknowledge, with thanks, contributions of the following individuals and entities that merged to produce the volume that you are presently reading.

Bryan Lewis   I have known Bryan for several years. He, in turn, is well aware of my devotion and loyalty to the Toronto Maple Leafs. On two occasions, I have asked him to lend his name and support to my writing projects, and he has responded both times without the slightest hesitation. I will always be grateful for his sincere encouragementof my writing ventures.

Pat Park   My initial contact with Pat came after I wrote a letter to Brian Burke, General Manager of the Leafs. Pat is the Director of Media Relations for the team, and he arranged a visit for me and my wife, Charlotte to the Leafs' practice facility in Etobicoke. Pat was there to greet us, and that occasion served its intended purpose of giving me insight into how an NHL team functions behind the scenes, in their working environment outside the glare of a game-day situation.

Colleen Magwood   Colleen is my daughter. She is a Primary Division teacher who works for the Halton District School Board at W. H. Morden Public School in Oakville, Ontario. She has had past work experience with computer graphics, and readily accepted my request to design the front and back covers for this book. She has also provided several sketches throughout the interior of the book.

Renal Staff – CVH   For the past ten years of my life, these people have played a major role in my life…in fact, they have sustained it. That is why it is my intent to donate all author's proceeds from sales of this book to support the work that they do. I have asked Ursula Betker, Acting Director of the Renal Department at Credit Valley Hospital, to provide my readers with a short summary of the operation of this very critical area of Ontario's Health Care System.

Trafford Publishing   Nine years ago, I contracted with Trafford to produce my first book about the Toronto Maple Leafs. I was very pleased with the fine work that they did in publishing **Heart and Spirit: The Toronto Maple Leafs of 2001 – 2002.** It seemed only logical to ask the same company to help me get my current effort, **Heart and Spirit Reborn**, into the hands of Leaf fans wherever they may be found. I eagerly await the finished product of our work together.

Family and Friends   My wife, Charlotte, along with our grown children, Colleen and Sean, have been steadfast supporters of my writing ever since I took up this pastime almost a decade ago. They all know how much I enjoy recording the everyday ventures of my favourite NHL team. Their hope is that in the very near future I will record for posterity the story of the next Leaf team to win the Stanley Cup. I am also very appreciative of the support afforded by many other family members and a tight circle of friends who have known of my steadfast interest in the Maple Leafs over the years.

I also wish to offer my thanks to the various publications and media outlets that impact my work directly and indirectly. Among these entities are:

- **The National Hockey League Official Guide & Record Book**
- **The Hockey News Yearbook**
- **The NHL Yearbook**
- **All NHL Internet Websites**
- **Wikepedia**
- **The Toronto Sports Media (Radio, Television & Print)**

Finally, the photographs used, both on the covers or inside the book have been taken by myself or provided with the authorization and/or approval of the subject(s) portrayed. The front cover shows both sides of a game-used puck given to me in the Spring of 2006 by Irene McCauley, whose son, Wes, officiated that game at the Air Canada Centre.

The opinions that you will read in this volume are my own, unless otherwise indicated. However, in order to express my viewpoints and convictions, I do my best to ensure that they are based upon the true facts that bear upon them. The sources outlined above are invaluable in my research tasks during the course of the writing process.

I sincerely hope that all of my readers enjoy the product of my efforts.

The Credit Valley Hospital Renal Program

Ursula Betker

The Renal Program at the Credit Valley Hospital in Mississauga, Ontario provides an interdisciplinary team approach to caring for patients with diminished kidney function and providing support when a patient's kidneys are no longer functioning adequately.

History of the Renal Program

Our dialysis unit started in 1985 with two nephrologists, a small peritoneal program and only a few hemodialysis patients. By 1986 the in-centre peritoneal dialysis moved to the hospital's nephrology unit and hemodialysis expanded. As the population of our community continued to grow, the hemodialysis unit continued to expand to meet the need. By 1999 the unit had expanded to 13 treatment stations. Shortly afterward, we added 25 more stations in the lower level of the hospital.

In December 2000, a partnership was established between the Credit Valley Hospital and Trillium Health Centre to provide acute dialysis to cardiac patients who develop renal failure following surgery. Within the first two years of initiating the service, the program provided hemodialysis to 111 patients and a proposal for expansion was developed.

The next ten years were challenging for the Renal Program as we faced a rapid growth in the need for services. This increased demand was driven by the tremendous growth in the local population. During this time we opened a satellite Renal Care Centre which became the new home for the Kidney Care Clinic, Home Care Peritoneal Clinic, and Home Hemodialysis and Transplant Follow up Clinics as well as 24 hemodialysis stations. When the hospital opened the Carlo Fidani Regional Cancer Centre in 2005, it provided space to house the Renal Program. This increased space enabled us to expand our services.

The Renal Program Today

Today, the Renal Program at the Credit Valley Hospital is a regional program that provides care for more than 850 patients each year. The following services are provided through three different locations:

- *Nephropathy Clinic:* The Nephropathy Clinic provides treatment for patients with early kidney disease. Its primary focus is promoting wellness, patient education and slowing down the progression of renal disease.
- *Kidney Care Clinic:* The Kidney Care Clinic provides a multi-disciplinary approach to delay the progression of kidney disease with advanced kidney failure. Education is provided as various methods of dialysis and transplant information is discussed to help prepare patients and families for the progression of chronic disease advances.
- *Transplant Follow*-up Clinic: Transplant Clinic provides care for renal transplant patients who have undergone a kidney transplant and require follow up care in their community.
- *Home Peritoneal Dialysis:* Home Peritoneal Dialysis Unit provides a support in an outpatient setting for patients that wish to maintain their independence by performing peritoneal dialysis in their home.
- *Home Hemodialysis:* Provides multi-disciplinary program care, education and support for those patients performing hemodialysis at home.
- *Hemodialysis:* Provides a total of 80 treatment stations at the hospital and the Renal Care Centre.
- *Inpatient Nephrology Patient Care Unit*

About The Credit Valley Hospital

The Credit Valley Hospital is a professional, caring, health care organization that promotes life, health and innovation. Credit Valley is known for its innovative approach to providing quality patient care to the people of Mississauga and the surrounding region (approximately one million people).

Credit Valley is the regional lead in specialized programs for clinical genetics, renal, maternal child care and oncology, as well as supporting programs in general medicine, surgery, emergency, mental health, complex continuing care, rehabilitation, obstetrics and gynaecology, paediatrics and cardiac services. The Mississauga Academy of Medicine (opening August of 2011) will be a partnership between the Faculty of Medicine at the University of Toronto, University of Toronto Mississauga, the Credit Valley Hospital and Trillium Health Centre.

Credit Valley supports the work of more than 4,700 staff, physicians, nurses and volunteers who handle over 700,000 patient visits to our location each year.

Credit Valley currently covers over one million square feet and is a 382-bed acute care inpatient facility, featuring a regional cancer and ambulatory care centre, a 24-hour emergency care centre and a regional women's and children's health centre featuring and advance level II neonatal intensive care unit and the largest paediatric oncology satellite program in Ontario outside of the Hospital for Sick Children (Toronto).

The Credit Valley Hospital has consistently met Accreditation Canada's national safety and patient care standards.

We wish to express our gratitude to Doug Magwood for the donation of proceeds from this book to supporting our Renal Program

Ursula Betker
Interim Patient Care Manager

July, 2011

Dedication

Irene McCauley

I wish to dedicate this book to the memory of Irene McCauley, a truly remarkable woman. Irene became a good friend of mine when we travelled together to Credit Valley Hospital in Mississauga over the course of seven years for dialysis treatments, the common consequence of kidney failure.

I first got to know Irene in the 1970's and 1980's, when she, her husband, John, and their three children, Wes, Blaine, and Bridgit were neighbours of the Magwoods on Greystone Crescent in Georgetown. At that time, John was a referee in the National Hockey League. He eventually rose to the position of Director of Officiating in the NHL, a post which he held from 1986 until his death in 1989.

In 1990, when I learned that I needed dialysis treatment to deal with my failing kidneys, I went to Irene for advice, knowing that she was also receiving her treatments at Credit Valley Hospital. For seven years after my dialysis sessions began, Irene and I both received our treatments at the same time on Thursday and Saturday evenings. Once a week, we travelled to CVH together.

I would describe Irene as a woman of very strong religious faith. She was a pillar of Holy Cross Roman Catholic Church in Georgetown. For more than two decades, she served as a trustee on the Halton District Separate School Board, representing the Town of Halton Hills.

As a young man, Irene's husband, John, was an elite athlete, excelling in both hockey and lacrosse. Irene herself came from an athletically inclined family. Her older sister, Winnie Roach Leuszler is well known as a pioneering Canadian marathon swimmer. In addition to her service as a school trustee, Irene retained many strong connections to a variety of sporting activities in both Halton and Peel.

In our travels together back and forth from CVH from 2001 to 2007, Irene and I talked a lot about the world of NHL hockey. She strongly supported my project of writing and publishing my first book, <u>Heart and Spirit: The Toronto Maple Leafs of 2001 – 2001: A Fan's Journal.</u> Hockey was an abiding interest for both of us, and we enjoyed exchanging anecdotes with one another.

Irene passed away in August of 2007. My family withheld news of her death from me for several days, since at the time I was recovering in CVH from a heart attack, and subsequent triple bypass surgery. I will always treasure the many hours of hockey talk that Irene and I shared during the "dialysis years".

Currently, John and Irene's son, Wes, has followed in his dad's footsteps, and is a referee in the National Hockey League. He lives in Portland, Maine with his wife and family. Their other son, Blaine, is a teacher with the HDSSB in Georgetown, and is well known in the local sporting community. Daughter, Bridgit and her family presently live in Kingston, Ontario.

The Leafs of 2010 - 2011

Introduction

Well, dear readers, Here I go again! Let me introduce myself.

My name is Doug Magwood. At this writing, I am seventy years of age…a retired educator who spent my career as an Elementary teacher, Vice-Principal, and Principal in what is presently known as the Regional Municipality of Halton. Since 1968, I have lived in Georgetown, Ontario. My wife, Charlotte, and I have raised two children. Our daughter, Colleen, is currently employed by the Halton District School Board as a Primary Division teacher, and our son, Sean, works for a well-known Industrial Equipment firm in nearby Mississauga.

I have been retired since March, 1991, when health issues became so severe that I was obliged to withdraw from my profession in the field of education. Since that time, I have been dealing with the consequences of diabetes, which I unfortunately contracted in 1965, at the age of twenty-five. The ravages of diabetes have affected my eyesight, my mobility, my heart, and my kidneys. In addition to all of my own problems, Charlotte, successfully overcame a bout with cancer and a severe urinary tract issue just a few years ago. In spite of all this, the Health Care System that we are blessed with here in Ontario has sustained us, and enabled us to enjoy a happy retirement. Although I would hesitate to describe the past few years of my life as "the Golden Years", Charlotte and I continue to enjoy our lives together, with the strong support of our family and a wonderful corps of friends.

Almost ten years ago, my deteriorating kidneys reached the point that I required dialysis, a life-sustaining procedure, in order to survive. Since then, I have travelled three times per week to Credit Valley Hospital in Mississauga, where each time I undergo a four-hour treatment on a dialysis machine in the Renal Unit.

Dialysis has further curtailed my retirement activities, and has kept me closer to home. I needed to find something to do…some sort of activity that would keep my mind occupied and at the same time be productive in some manner or another.

I decided to write a book. That book would be about the Toronto Maple Leafs. I would have the book published, and I would donate any and all profits acquired to the Renal Unit at Credit Valley Hospital. My writing would not be for any personal monetary gain whatsoever. My entire satisfaction would be achieved by accomplishing the goal of completing my book, and possibly benefiting others at the conclusion of the exercise.

I am happy to report that my goals were accomplished. In the Fall of 2002, Trafford Publishing, of Victoria, B. C. published my book, entitled **Heart and Spirit: A Fan's Journal of the 2001 - 2002 Toronto Maple Leafs.** I was honoured that Ron Ellis, a member of the 1967 Stanley Cup Champion Maple Leafs agreed to write the foreword of the book. A good friend, Bryan Lewis, former Director of Officiating for the NHL, also wrote a page endorsing my project. Another acquaintance, Ted Brown, an outstanding photographer and writer for the Georgetown Independent & Free Press, looked after some photography and cover design with the capable assistance of Kevin Powell, a co-worker at the newspaper.

My book did not make a significant profit. I was able to cover the amount of money that it cost me to have the book published, but not much more. I was able to make a small donation to Credit Valley Hospital, and I donated several books to use in the CVH Foundation's annual fund-raising auction. I was told that my publisher charged too much for shipments to bookstores in Eastern Canada, therefore my book did not get distributed to stores in the Greater Toronto Area. Had that happened, I am confident that sales would have been significantly higher, and the CVH Renal Unit would have benefited accordingly. Live and Learn. For this book, which will record Leaf history throughout the 2010 - 2011 NHL season, I will only sign with a company that will GUARANTEE distribution throughout the GTA.

All of the above brings me to the present time. Today is the 27th day of August, 2010. As each day passes, the Sports media increasingly directs our attention to hockey. This week, a major conference took place in Toronto. Some of the greatest minds in hockey, both amateur and professional, met to discuss the place that hockey holds in the world today. The state of the game was reviewed, and discussion included matters both positive and negative which are dealt with by administrators the world over who work in this great sport on a daily basis. Perhaps in years to come, such conferences will be held regularly, and our great and beloved game will grow internationally, and reach millions more fans as the years go on.

Within a couple of weeks, all teams in the National Hockey League will convene their annual training camps. As this is written, clubs are signing available players to help fill out rosters in both the NHL clubs, their AHL farm team affiliates, and other feeder leagues throughout North America.

Another exciting season will soon begin, and once again the Toronto Maple Leafs will try to fulfill a dream that fans like myself have longed for since 1967...**the return of the Stanley Cup to one of the most glorious franchises in the history of professional sports.**

Good luck to everyone who has a role to play in achieving this great objective.

Doug Magwood
Georgetown, Ontario

August 2010

__Prologue__

One cold, blustery Saturday night, fifty-eight years ago this winter, I watched my first NHL game on television. For years, families across Canada and beyond have gathered around their radios and listened to the unforgettable voice of Foster Hewitt on "Hockey Night in Canada". Beginning in 1952, the legendary hockey broadcast had made the leap to television. Every Saturday evening, beginning at 8:00 P.M. the CBC broadcast Leaf games from Maple Leaf Gardens, joining the games "in progress".

In 1952, not a lot of people in the little Ontario town of Fergus had television. I can clearly remember the name of the first family in town to have a TV set. The Findleys lived on Union Street, and I have a clear recollection of the day that my dad drove us down that street just to see what a television antenna looked like.

Before long, several other families in town had purchased television sets. One of my schoolmates, Morley Richardson, belonged to one such family, and he had invited a couple of us over to his place to watch the hockey game on that chilly winter's evening.

I was hooked! From that night on, I was a hockey fan. More specifically...**I was a Toronto Maple Leaf Hockey fan!**

For almost six decades, I have cheered for the Toronto Maple Leafs. I am objective enough to admire and appreciate the greatness of other teams and other players, but my true loyalty has **__never__** wavered from the Maple Leafs.

For the first eighteen seasons of following the Maple Leafs, the franchise experienced a degree of success that significantly added to the legendary status of the club. In that period, the Leafs won FIVE Stanley Cups, and only missed the playoffs three times. Since that last cup, though, there have been more than four decades of negativism and drift. The team faltered significantly during the reign of the infamous Harold Ballard, and it has suffered for years as the result of poor management. Sixteen times the Leafs have failed to qualify for the post-season tournaments.

There have been a few teams that have thrilled us, engendering hope of success on sporadic occasions, but sadly, that hope flickered out like the passing of a shooting star. Great leaders, such as Sundin, Gilmour, Clark and Sittler have dazzled us with their talents and on-ice inspirational leadership, but all of them never experienced the thrill of hoisting the cup as a Maple Leaf. Perhaps Dion Phaneuf will be destined to fulfill that dream.

Over the course of the past nine years, I have written books about each Maple Leaf season. In my Introduction, I told you about the only one that has been published to date. Seven others have been written, but, as we all know, the team has endured a period of hard times. For the past five years, the Leaf seasons have ended at the conclusion of the regular NHL schedule. To be bluntly honest, the Maple Leafs have failed at several levels as a professional sports franchise, and therefore hockey fans would justifiably find little about the team to warrant buying a book that relates such doom and gloom. Consequently, seven of my books are gathering dust in my computer room.

It is my sincere hope that THIS book will be different. I have had an initial discussion with a publishing company with close ties to bookshops in the Greater Toronto Area…a population base of more than three million souls, many of whom have a deep and abiding interest in the Toronto Maple Leafs.

This year's team shows promise. It is being managed by Brian Burke, who was hired a couple of years ago for the sole purpose of rebuilding the hockey franchise and returning the Stanley Cup to Toronto after an absence of forty-three years. Since his arrival, Brian has brought in management personnel to help him forge and work towards objectives that will render successful outcomes. He has been a close friend of his head coach, Ron Wilson, for many years. Last year, Brian and Ron guided the USA Olympic Team to a silver medal at the Vancouver Olympics. Brian has also made several significant changes with the Maple Leaf roster. He traded away draft picks in order to acquire Phil Kessel from the Boston Bruins. Kessel is expected to be a forty-goal scorer for the next several seasons. He made another major trade last year to acquire Dion Phaneuf from the Calgary Flames. Phaneuf is a big, strong defenceman with significant leadership capabilities, Just a few weeks ago, Phaneuf was named team captain, succeeding the great Mats Sundin, whose departure from the Leafs left a huge void in the club's leadership.

Since the arrival of Brian Burke in Toronto, things are beginning to look up. As the old saying goes, Rome wasn't built in a day. The Toronto Maple Leafs will also require a period of time to reach the capability of winning a Stanley Cup. I have a feeling that we are going to see some more progress towards that goal throughout the coming season. We will see an evolutionary process as the season unfolds, and I will do my very best to outline that process in great detail.

Maple Leafs Name Dion Phaneuf as Captain

In a media conference at 3 o'clock this afternoon, Brian Burke, President and General Manager of the Toronto Maple Leafs, along with Head Coach Ron Wilson, announced that Dion Phaneuf had accepted the position as Captain of the hockey club.

Phaneuf posed awkwardly for a few pictures with Wilson, then donned a spiffy new jersey that will be worn by the Leafs when they take to the ice in October for the 2010 - 2011 NHL season.

Sharing the podium with Phaneuf were three legendary former Leaf captains, George Armstrong, Darryl Sittler, and Wendel Clark. Seated in the front row of the assembled audience were several members of the Maple Leaf Board of Directors along with current Leaf players Tyler Bozak, Luke Schenn, and Phil Kessel.

An observer would be reasonably accurate in suggesting that the four Leaf players on hand at this ceremony were symbolic of the main qualities that the coming season's team are expected to portray…size, toughness, speed, and scoring acumen. Both Phaneuf and Luke Schenn are big men, and they will both patrol the blue line. It is going to be an expectation that they will be hard to play against. Tyler Bozak, on the other hand, is of smaller physical stature, but a player who has already begun to impress both management and fans with speed and accuracy in passing the puck. Phil Kessel is the sniper amongst those present today. He was acquired by Brian Burke last year for one reason…goal production. He lived up to that expectation in 2009 - 2010 by scoring thirty goals in a season that was shortened by a full month to allow him to recuperate from injury. He will need to score at least forty times in the coming season, or he will fall short of a successful standard.

Last week, the Chicago Blackhawks won the Stanley Cup. They did so by following a recipe that appears to be a good part of Brian Burke's vision for the Leafs. Youth, speed, defensive toughness, sound goalkeeping, and a potent offence up front will be central to Leaf success in their impending campaign.

It is mid-June, as this is written. Over the course of the next two weeks, Brian Burke and his cohorts in the Leaf front office will be carefully planning a course of action for improving the Leafs by way of the trade market and/or free agency. Those two avenues will afford Burke the opportunities he needs to solidify a team whose sole objective for the coming season will be **making the playoffs in the Spring of 2011.**

Today, Dion Phaneuf accepted the challenge and responsibility of leading the Toronto Maple Leafs to that objective.

Good Luck, Dion! ALL LEAF FANS WISH YOU NOTHING BUT THE BEST!

Leaf Rookie Tournament Gets the Season Under Way

For the past few days, there has been a touch of Autumn in the air. After a summer that has been described as one of the hottest on record, we have all been somewhat taken aback by a spate of sharply cool mornings. In the offices and rinks operating under the direction of the Toronto Maple Leafs, weather is the last thing to occupy the brain trust of this storied NHL franchise. All thoughts are centred upon the beginning stages of the 2010 -2011 NHL season…one that promises to be critical in the resurgence of the Leafs back into serious contention for the Stanley Cup.

Twenty-eight names appear on the roster of players for this year's rookie tournament. There are three goalies, ten defencemen, and fifteen forwards. These players range in age from eighteen to twenty five, and represent at least nine major hockey organizations in North America and Europe. Of these players, few, if any will see much action with this season's parent club. Many of them, though, will eventually be assigned to Leaf farm clubs in the AHL, continue Junior terms in the Ontario Hockey League (OHL), , the Western Hockey League (WHL) the Quebec Major Junior Hockey League (QMJHL), or continue playing for a University-based team in the USA.

Every one of the players involved in the rookie tournament will be under close scrutiny by scouts employed by any number of NHL organizations. These players have been scouted for years…ever since most of them were little boys. All of them have dreams of making the NHL. Indeed, they are ALMOST there. In this tournament, they are wearing the uniforms of an NHL club, and I am sure that their every family photo album will forever be adorned by images of these boys attaining the elite level of their sport, However, the reality will be that only a handful will ever wear those colours for more than a brief span of their careers. Thousands of young people aspire to play hockey in the NHL, but the reality is that only about seven hundred secure that level of accomplishment at any given time.

This year's rookie tournament will involve the Leafs, the Chicago Blackhawks and the Pittsburgh Penguins. The games are being played in London, Ontario at the John Labatt Centre.

Training camp for the Toronto Maple Leafs will begin this coming Friday, September 17th. From that day forward, the long and strenuous trek to the Stanley Cup playoffs will begin in earnest. The ensuing two weeks will see the initial roster evolve, and when the first puck drops on October 7th, we will all know the players who will band together to lift this great hockey organization out of the abyss of the past five seasons, and back to the glory that we have all missed so badly for so many years.

Leaf Training Camp Begins

This morning, beginning at 9:00 A.M., sixty-three professional hockey players assembled in Etobicoke, on Kipling Avenue, to begin formal training at the annual Toronto Maple Leaf training camp.

Right off the bat, they will all be subjected to a barrage of tests and examinations by the medical staff engaged by Leaf management in order to assess each player's medical status and fitness levels. This initial stage will be critical for any player who has had his career impacted within the past few months by either injury or illness. Mike Komisarek comes to mind. Last year, he missed a significant portion of the season due to an arm injury. This was particularly frustrating for him, since it was his first year as a Leaf, having been signed to a lucrative contract by Toronto after several successful seasons with the Montreal Canadiens. Jeff Finger, Phil Kessel, and Jonas Gustavsson also were confronted by medical issues during the 2009-2010 season, They will be anxious to get medical clearance for the new campaign that looms just a couple of weeks away.

Of the players assembling this morning, only a couple of dozen will emerge wearing the colours of the parent club. Several of the youngest among them will eventually return to teams at the Junior and University levels. Others, still showing that they possess potential in the professional ranks, will be assigned to farm teams in the American Hockey League or another such league in the USA. A very few camp participants may either be traded, or perhaps even advised that their playing days at this level are over.

The players whose levels of skill rank closest to the elite level required in the NHL will, in all likelihood, be posted to the Toronto Marlies, whose home arena is the Ricoh Coliseum, just a few short blocks from the Air Canada Centre.

The next couple of weeks will unfold for all the players in camp with head-spinning speed. In a very compressed time period, there will be physical workouts, both on and off the ice. There will be nine exhibition games played against a handful of other NHL teams, and, as all these events unfold, the coaching and management staff will be making critical decisions that will profoundly affect the development of the Leafs as a team as well as the individual career paths of a considerable number of the players on the training camp roster.

For the record, then, here are the players aspiring to be team members of the Toronto Maple Leafs during the 2010-2011 NHL season.

* INCUMBENT PLAYERS ARE INDICATED IN BOLDFACE PRINT

Goaltenders (6)

Andrew Engelage	**Jean Sebastien Giguere**	**Jonas Gustavsson**
James Reimer	Jussi Rynnas	Ben Scrivens

Defence (19)

Keith Aulie	**Francois Beauchemin**	Jessie Blacker
Mike Brennan	Josh Engel	**Jeff Finger**
Carl Gunnarsson	Simon Gysbers	Korbinian Holzer
Tomas Kaberle	**Mike Komisarek**	Matt Lashoff
Brett Lebda	Juraj Mikus	Drew Paris
Dion Phaneuf "C"	Danny Richmond	**Luke Schenn**
Barron Smith		

Forwards (39)

Colby Armstrong	Darryl Boyce	**Tyler Bozak**
Tim Brent	Mike Brown	**Luca Caputi**
Sam Carrick	Joey Crabb	Andrew Crescenzi
Jerry D'Amigo	Jamie Devane	Alex Foster
Mikhail Grabovski	Richard Greenop	Ryan Hamilton
Christian Hanson	Justin Hodgman	Brayden Irwin
Nazem Kadri	**Phil Kessel**	**Nikolai Kulemin**
Mike Liambas	Clarke MacArthur	Greg McKegg
Dale Mitchell	**John Mitchell**	Marcel Mueller
Josh Nicholls	**Colton Orr**	**Jay Rosehill**
Brad Ross	Ken Ryan	Gregg Scott
Fredrik Sjostrom	Robert Slaney	Mikhail Stefanovich
Kris Versteeg	Mike Zigomanis	Wayne Primeau

Hitting the Ice

Yesterday, for the players gathered at the Mastercard Centre for Hockey Excellence, was a day focussed upon two main activities. First and foremost was enduring the poking, prodding, and other numerous physical demands of the medical and training staff employed by the Toronto Maple Leafs to assess the preparedness of all candidates for the approximately two dozen roster spots on the team. Secondly, the players were obliged to don their spanking, new uniforms for media photographs and interviews. Several players are obviously used to those routines, while others are less comfortable in the glare of the media circus. However, one thing is certain. Any player intent upon wearing the famous blue and white of the Maple Leafs had better get used to such scrutiny, because in Toronto it comes with the territory.

The focus of today's activities will be entirely different. The players will be on the ice in full uniform. The coaches will be putting them through a regimen of drills and situations designed to bring out the levels of competence that will be required to secure a place on the team. But.......what team?

At his media scrum yesterday, head coach Ron Wilson clearly stated that, by next Sunday, the 26th, he wanted the parent club, the Leafs, pared down to what he called a "manageable number". That number will be somewhere in the neighbourhood of 24 to 26. Who, of the 64 bodies currently in camp, will find themselves in the Maple Leaf dressing room, pulling on the jersey emblazoned with THE big leaf on the front?

At this writing, there are at least fifteen players on the Maple Leafs who are being paid a minimum of $ 1,000,000 for the impending hockey season. While a player's salary is not a guarantee of a spot on the team, it is reasonable to assume that if management is paying an individual in excess of a million bucks, said player is expected to perform on the ice at a skill level high enough to warrant that amount. If one does the math, we can all see that there aren't very many vacancies up for grabs.

There will not be a lot of rookies on the final Leaf roster when the regular season begins. I would suggest that two or three at the very most is all that the Leafs can afford. The precarious position that the team is in...having failed to make the playoffs in five consecutive seasons... demands that Wilson and his staff ice a club that is fully aware of the heavy demands required for competitive success in the NHL. Starting today, every player on the training camp roster will be scrutinized like they probably have never been before. The decisions made by Leaf coaches and managers over the course of the next two or three weeks will profoundly impact the careers of dozens of players, for many years to come.

My Advice to Young Hockey Players …(and Others)

If there is an over-riding impression of the players currently in attendance at this year's Toronto Maple Leaf training camp it is their <u>youthfulness.</u> There is only a handful of players whose ages exceed 30. Goalie J. S. Giguere is 33. Defencemen Francois Beauchemin and Jeff Finger are both 30. Tomas Kaberle is 32. The average age of all forwards listed on the roster is 24.6 The team's new Captain, Dion Phaneuf is just 25. In other words, dear readers, most of the current crop of Maple Leafs have their careers ahead of them.

Next week, I will be 71 years of age. I have been an active observer of life in the NHL for more than half a century. From this vantage point, I believe that I am in a position to offer these young men, and any others who may be reading my work, some words of advice that could potentially lead them to successful and productive careers in the world of professional hockey. So…here goes!

First and foremost, there is a single quality to which ANYONE should direct their life performance. That quality is **<u>INTEGRITY.</u>** The dictionary defines integrity as:

1. adherence to moral principles; honest
2. the quality of being unimpaired; soundness
3. Unity; wholeness

In my personal career, I spent 18 years as an Elementary School Principal. An important part of my job was that of evaluating teachers, and to that end, I received a great deal of training in order to do an effective job of it. Over the years, I came to the conclusion that, above all of the various individual skills and qualities that people brought to bear in their chosen occupation, personal integrity stood out above everything. I did not always agree with positions taken by others who worked with me in the field of education, but I was able to respect and appreciate that their stance on issues was every bit as valid as mine. They possessed honest and sound beliefs that could be objectively viewed with respect. Such people, in my opinion, epitomized personal integrity, and I have always admired them as colleagues in my chosen profession.

Any young athlete who rises to successful levels in his or her sport will, in all likelihood, be a person who is regarded as someone with a very high level of integrity. That level of respect is something that will evolve over a considerable number of years. In addition, there are other aspects of personal and career development that require a high degree of awareness for success and fulfillment.

I would like to exclusively reserve my next comments to the "arena" of amateur and professional sports. My advice is based upon both personal observations and media reports of real events relating to real people. Young people aspiring to careers in the world of sports need to avoid certain temptations that will inevitably confront them. Those temptations are:

1. Booze   2. Drugs   3. Lust (Personal and Material)

The evils of alcohol are well documented throughout history. Most adults, certainly those of my age, can conjure up the names of people in many walks of life whose careers and personal lives have been adversely impacted by alcohol. When alcohol use reaches the stage of addiction in anyone's life, the likelihood of negative consequences frequently becomes reality. The extreme consequences of alcohol abuse are ruination, and even death. Alcohol abuse in the early years of adulthood is **WITHOUT EXCEPTION**, bad news. In hockey, the practice of enjoying a couple of "pops" following a game is almost a tradition, but even that more or less "recreational" consumption can lead to trouble. In his book **Shooting for Glory**, Paul Henderson tells the stories of a couple of his Maple Leaf team-mates whose experiences with alcohol can only be characterized as harrowing.

The impact of drugs represents another scourge in the field of sports and athletics. Just a couple of weeks ago, a young Canadian football player was identified as being the first competitive athlete in North America to be tested positive for human growth hormones. What kind of fame and distinction does that diagnosis bring him? In the USA, the use of performance enhancing drugs in Major League Baseball has resulted in the impending convening of a congressional committee that could result in prison time for legendary pitcher Roger Clemens. Other players have forfeited inclusion in the Hall of Fame as a result of their drug use.

We are all aware that lust is one of the seven deadly sins. In the current era of vast media coverage of professional sports, we have seen athletes achieve great personal wealth by way of winning huge amounts of prize money in their sport, and in addition signing lucrative contracts with multiple sponsors. Tiger Woods, blessed with incredible skill as a golfer, over time became a billionaire. All of his money provided him with every resource he needed to lust after even more material and monetary possessions. It has been revealed that he has been a well-known "high roller" in Las Vegas for years. Sadly, Woods allowed his lust to become personal, at the expense of his seemingly pristine family life. His lust for the good life has backfired. His success on the golf course has taken a major hit. He has lost his wife, and has to share custody of his children for the rest of their childhood. He has to pay a small fortune in alimony to his ex-wife, and several of his most lucrative sponsors have abandoned him. His integrity is in tatters. Lust has brought all this upon him.

At the risk of being accused of preaching, I honestly believe that ANY aspiring athlete should wisely observe the advice that I have inscribed on these two pages.

Training Camp - Interim Report

This morning, we awake to the news that the Toronto Maple Leaf training camp roster has been trimmed to the "manageable number" that Ron Wilson set as his objective a week ago, when the camp opened. Remaining and competing for spots on the final contingent are 3 goalies, 10 defencemen, and 17 forwards.

The Leafs played five games on consecutive nights last week, winning two and losing three, one by way of a shootout. There have been two major cuts to the massive group of 63 that were on hand a week or so ago. Players have been assigned to the Marlies, sent back to Junior clubs, or returned to college teams. Two players, Mike Liambas and Wayne Primeau, were released outright from their try-out contracts.

Between tonight and next Saturday, the Leafs will play four more "friendlies" against Buffalo (1), Ottawa (1), and Detroit (2). Ron Wilson and his staff will be paying very close attention to line combinations and defence pairings. Their eventual decisions about final cuts will be crucial in terms of icing the strongest possible team when the opening puck drops on October 7th.

As far as the goalies are concerned, it is clear that Giguere and Gustavsson will be suiting up for the Leafs when the season begins. Jamie Reimer will eventually be assigned to the Marlies, but will stay with the Leafs to spell off the other two until the exhibition games have concluded.

On defence, the Leafs are strong. The next four games will serve to clarify who is best suited to be paired with whom. I would suggest that Beauchemin, Kaberle, Komisarek, Phaneuf, and Schenn all have a lock on a final roster spot, while the coaching staff will have a job on their hands sorting out rankings for Finger, Gunnarsson, Lashoff, Lebda, and Richmond. I still believe that Brian Burke and his staff will be waiting for the phone to ring with a substantial offer for Tomas Kaberle. If such an offer materializes, I am sure that they will do their best to persuade Tomas to move on. I really don't think that Kaberle is a part of Burke's long-term vision for the Leafs.

As far as the forwards are concerned, there are still some decisions about who merit's a spot on the Leafs, and who should be posted to the Marlies. John Mitchell has not had a particularly good camp, and may be "on the bubble". The same could be argued about Nazim Kadri, who has clearly struggled during the exhibition games that have been played. Even though the next four games mean nothing in the overall scheme of things, the impact that they might have upon individual careers MAY be of consequence.

Good luck down the stretch, boys!

Training Camp Ends - A Final Report

This morning, training camps across the entire NHL have come to an end. It is reported today that the Toronto Maple Leafs had a bit of a celebration following Saturday evening's final pre-season win over the Detroit Red Wings. Later today, Brian Burke will undoubtedly be issuing a media release announcing the final cuts from the training camp roster. I will await his decisions before I make any specific comments.

****

While the exhibition games held in the pre-season ultimately mean little or nothing in the overall scheme of things, they do afford the coaching and management staff of a team a glimpse of what the club MAY look like as the coming season unwinds. As well, people like myself, who have followed a team religiously over the years, are afforded the opportunity to formulate an assessment about the possibilities that our favourite franchise may possess come playoff time next Spring.

I am optimistic about this year's Toronto Maple Leafs. I base my optimism upon what I have observed AND recorded as training camp and the exhibition schedule have transpired. Here is a short summary of my observations and thoughts.

THE LEAFS WILL MAKE THE PLAYOFFS THIS SEASON. They won 5 games in pre-season play, and lost 4. They accumulated 11 of a possible 18 points. That works out to a winning percentage of 61.1%. If they had achieved that mark last year, the Leafs would have wound up in **THIRD PLACE** in the Eastern Conference. For that reason, I feel confident that a playoff position is achievable this year.

Point Production will undergo a significant upturn as the current season progresses. The pre-season exhibition schedule also has engendered a good degree of optimism about the Leafs' scoring capabilities this year. In 9 games, the Leafs scored 27 goals...an average of 3 per game. Last year's team was hard-pressed to manage 2.5. Scoring distribution through the pre-season was also interesting. Here is a chart that shows some interesting features:

Position	Goals	Assists	Points
Centre	8	8	16
Left Wing	7	8	15
Right Wing	10	14	24
Defence	2	18	20
AVERAGES	3	5.3	8.3

8.3   X   82   =   683.3

Last year's Leafs scored 214 goals. If we project, for this season, an average of 3 goals per game, they will score 246. If they had scored such a total throughout 2009 - 2010, the Leafs would have been the third highest scoring team in the Eastern Conference.

The Leafs are definitely going to need more scoring strength this year, and Brian Burke has deliberately acquired players whom he feels can deliver. A detailed analysis of the nine exhibition games provides some hints about which players will be expected to take much of the responsibility for a bit of a surge in point production.

Position	Player	Goals	Assists	Points
Centre	Grabovski	2	4	6
Centre	Bozak	2	2	4
Left Wing	Kulemin	5	1	6
Left Wing	MacArthur	1	4	5
Right Wing	Kessel	6	4	10
Right Wing	Versteeg	2	7	9
Defence	Phaneuf	1	5	6
Defence	Kaberle	1	3	4

The above eight players are going to be counted upon to "carry the mail". Two of them (MacArthur and Versteeg) are new to the team this year. Bozak, Kessel and Phaneuf were on hand for portions of the 09-10 season. Grabovski, Kulemin, and Kaberle were on the roster for the full year, although Grabovski missed 23 games due to injury.

It is also worthy for me to point out that my chart on the previous page shows a very nice balance in point production at all four positions.

To summarize, then, I believe that once this year's Leaf team becomes accustomed to playing with one another, and becomes acclimatized with the new personnel and the qualities that each brings to the ice, we **should** be able to anticipate post-season play for the first time in half a decade.

****

3:00 P.M.

The final Maple Leaf cuts from the training camp roster have been posted on the Internet. They are as follows:

Assigned to the Marlies

Luca Caputi	Christian Hanson	Nazem Kadri	Jussi Rynnas

Placed on Waivers

Danny Richmond	Jay Rosehill	Mike Zigomanis

October 6, 2010

The Kaberle Factor - A Potential "Fly in the Ointment?"

Everything in the media today pretty well reflects all the good things that are expected from this year's Maple Leafs.

Rah! Rah! Rah!…..Sis!…..Boom!…..Bah!

Perhaps that's the way that things should be projected on the day before the new season begins. I most certainly count myself as an optimist as the new season approaches, and I fervently hope that my optimism is fulfilled by a young and exciting Leaf team. However, something happened yesterday that bothers me…more than just a little.

I have just finished watching Ron Wilson's interview with the media yesterday following the team practice. About half-way through, he was asked to identify this season's alternate captains. He abruptly answered that Beauchemin and Komisarek would wear the "A" on their sweaters. "Not Kaberle?" "No, just those two. Period."

Nothing more was said about the alternate captains.

That bothers me.

Tomas Kaberle has been an alternate captain of the Toronto Maple Leafs ever since the NHL lockout. That was five full seasons ago. Yet, in a terse announcement, unembellished by any comment at all, Kaberle is no longer acknowledged as a team leader.

If that isn't being FIRED from the job, then you tell me what it is!

I have stated earlier in this work that I believe Tomas Kaberle does not fit into Brian Burke's future plans for the Maple Leafs. For months, Burke has tried to rid the team of the veteran defenceman. The words of William Shakespeare come to mind…"Out! Out! Damned Spot!" The first obstacle that Burke had to deal with was Kaberle's "no-trade" contract clause. The second was undoubtedly his substantial salary figure of $ 4, 125,000. I would also think that the latter of those factors underlie the reality that there have been no acceptable offers for Tomas's services to date.

Then, midway through this summer, a media report from the Czech Republic quoted Kaberle's father, saying that Tomas would never sign another contract with the Leafs as long as Ron Wilson was the head coach. That quote raised more than a few eyebrows, and was assuredly unhelpful. Tomas's only response to this situation was that he was not able to control what his father had to say.

Today, there was a clip on television during which Tomas stated that losing the "A" on his jersey was not a big deal to him. It was simply the coach's call, and he was all right with that.

Frankly, I don't believe him.

If I had been the assistant captain of the Maple Leafs for the past six years, and suddenly that role was taken from me in such an arbitrary manner, It would certainly be a big deal. Think about the current situation for a minute:

- each NHL team is allowed **one Captain** and **three Assistants**
- The Leaf coach has decided upon **one Captain** and **two Assistants**
- **NOT ONE** of the Captain or the two Assistants have yet played s full season with the team that they now lead.

The Kaberle situation, as it presently exists, clearly indicates that the Leafs and their veteran defenceman are NOT on the same page. I would even venture the opinion that there is a bit of "game playing" going on, with both parties being complicit.

Let's get real. The Leafs don't want Kaberle on the team any more. Brian Burke (with the support of the Leaf Board of Directors, I'm sure) is unwilling to buy out his contract (a la Darcy Tucker) and lose Kaberle to another team, receiving nothing in return. Kaberle is fully aware that he is not welcome, and will stay in Toronto until some team, desperately in need of his skills, comes calling, and offers him another contract…**AND** A MULTI-YEAR EXTENSION.

Until then, Tomas will be a good little boy, and put up with a nasty situation comforted to some degree each time he lines up to collect his big. fat paycheque.

****

Tomorrow night, the Maple Leafs open the season by hosting their long-time rivals, the Montreal Canadiens. At the first drop of the puck, the quest for a post-season berth begins. Every game is important. Every point is valuable. Every Leaf player is under the microscope.

I am optimistic about the coming season. In my writing, I will do my level best to be objective. At the same time, I intend to be brutally honest in my opinions concerning events that happen as the campaign unfolds.

I am sick of the Toronto Maple Leafs losing record. Things must turn around NOW!

Accountability at every level of the Maple Leaf organization is on the line.

The future begins NOW!

Leafs Nip Montreal in Home Opener

Well, the Leafs got off to a reasonably good start for the new NHL campaign last night with a well-earned win over the Canadiens. The final score was a pretty good indication of the play. It was an entertaining game from start to finish. With the victory, Toronto was awarded two of the three stars for the event.

Jean Sebastien Giguere was undoubtedly a good choice for the first star. He made two or three saves as the third period wound down, and prevented the visitors from potting a goal that would have sent the game into overtime.

Clarke MacArthur took the puck off the sideboards, skated full bore towards Carey Price in the Montreal net, and blazed a backhander into the net. His marker proved to be the winner.

The other Leaf goals were scored by Phil Kessel and newcomer Tim Brent, who hails from nearby Cambridge Ontario.

The Leafs showed last night that this year's team is capable of playing an up-tempo game, and sustain it for three full periods. That is undoubtedly attributable to the youth of the team, coupled with an elevated awareness of how important it is going to be for the club to have a good month of October. As we can all recall only too well, last year's start amounted to a disaster. The Leafs only won a single game during October, and for all intents and purposes, their season was over. They simply didn't have the horses to recover.

If there was indeed anything to be critical about in this game, it was the matter of turnovers. I can recall a graphic on my television screen at one point indicating that the Habs had turned the puck over 4 times, and the Leafs had done so on 10 occasions. That sort of thing has to be corrected. I am confident that once the Leafs get a few more games under their belts, they will be able to control the puck more skillfully, and perform at a higher level of efficiency.

To conclude, it was essential that the Leafs performed well in last night's inaugural match. They succeeded, and their fans all went home happy. Those of us who watched the game on "Hockey Night in Canada" could not help but be encouraged by what we saw.

Next up is another important match-up on Saturday evening, when the so-called "Battle of Ontario" resumes. The Ottawa Senators will take to the Air Canada Centre ice, and I anticipate that the game will have significant meaning for both teams. It should be a very interesting evening of hockey, indeed.

Leaf Impressive Over Sens in Battle of Ontario

The Maple Leafs are off to their best start since 1999 as a result of posting their second consecutive win in as many games last night. This game, the first in this season's "Battle of Ontario" was no contest. The Leafs took a 2 - 0 lead in the first period and never looked back. Nikolai Kulemin scored his first of the season at the 1:38 mark of the opening period, and Phil Kessel wristed a shot past Pascal Leclaire to set the visitors back on their heels.

Clarke MacArthur got his second goal of the season in the middle frame, The home team notched two more in the third from Kris Versteeg and Tim Brent, giving the Leafs a commanding 5 - 0 lead.

The only Senators goal was scored by Jason Spezza, who was playing his first game of the year, having missed his home opener due to a slight groin injury. You could sense his frustration at his team's situation as he skated brusquely to the Senator's bench scowling and barely celebrating his sure-fire goal when the puck took an odd bounce off the boards giving Giguere no chance for a save.

The Leafs looked powerful last night. They outshot the Senators by a margin of 38 to 18. Giguere only had to handle 6 shots in each of the three periods. The only Ottawa goal was a bit of a fluke, or else he would have posted a shutout. I was extremely impressed by the way the Leafs all came back into their own end to help defend against the Senators when they were on the attack. They were truly playing as a team.

The three stars of the game were MacArthur, Versteeg, and Kessel. All three players posted two points apiece.

The Senators have gotten off to a very disappointing start. They have lost both of their opening matches, one at home and one on the road. They looked disorganized. They lacked energy. The body language of the players, their head coach, and their General Manager showed clearly that nobody is happy with the present posture of the team.

Next week, the Leafs travel to Pittsburgh and New York to play their first two road games against the Penguins and the Rangers. They return home to entertain the Islanders the following Monday. By this time next week, we should have a fairly clear idea about just how promising this year's Leafs are going to be.

So far…so good!

Leafs Prevail Over Stumbling Penguins

Pinch me! I must be dreaming!

The Toronto Maple Leafs have posted victories in their first three games of the season. This hasn't happened for more than a decade. Although it is still FAR too early to start making outlandish predictions about the fate of this year's club, it sure feels good to look over team statistics that have established a 100% level of achievement.

Thus far, this year's Leafs can be described as a "feel good" team. They look determined as they file out onto the ice at the beginning of the game. They look confident. There is certainly a youthful exuberance emanating from the group, and that has been the result of Brian Burke's deliberate plan on icing a group of players that can eventually be expected to produce a winning team whose success will hopefully extend for several years into the future.

Last night, the Leafs stormed out and took control of the game right away. They got the first goal on a deflection off the stick of Colton Orr. The Penguins eventually got their bearings shortly after the mid-point of the period and began to take the play away from the Leafs. They got goals from Kunitz and Talbot, and skated off for the first intermission with a one-goal lead.

Toronto asserted their dominance in the second period, and racked up three goals from Francois Beauchemin and Clarke MacArthur (2). The latter has gotten off to a blistering start, having scored four goals in his first three games as a Leaf. The emergence of unexpected scoring prowess from players other than those known to possess superior skills around the net could bode well for the future. Opposing teams will have to pay more attention to these so-called "lesser lights", and the end result MIGHT give more room to the well-known snipers such as Kessel, Kulemin and Grabovski.

Ron Wilson gave last night's start in goal to Jonas Gustavsson. He played a good game, and made some key saves, particularly in the third period, when the Pens were doing their best to tie the game. Thus far, both he and Giguere have provided good, solid performances, so the Leafs can gradually become more and more confident that this year's goaltending is not going to be as serious an issue as it was early last year.

If there was a disappointing aspect of last night's game, it would have to be the Leafs' shots-on-goal production. They only managed 14 shots on Fleury in the Pittsburgh net. Normally, a low shot total like that would end up with a loss. I'm sure that Ron Wilson will do his best to correct that aspect of his team's performance before they take on the Rangers at Madison Square Gardens tomorrow night.

Kessel Leads Leafs to Overtime Victory.

I am furious! I am absolutely livid! For some people who watched last night's game between the Leafs and the Rangers, an incident took place that MAY have gone almost unnoticed. However, the nasty exchange that occurred involving Mike Komisarek and Sean Avery WAS captured on-camera, even though the two players were some distance away from the main action being focused upon.

Now, I don't know what Mike Komisarek said to Avery. It really doesn't matter, because I probably couldn't print the words here anyway. Still, **no verbal exchange, in my mind, could justify what Sean Avery did in response! He used his stick like a baseball bat, and two-handed Komisarek on the legs…not once…BUT TWICE!** Komisarek fell to the ice in pain.

The point of my outrage is this. From the time that kids are introduced to the game of hockey, they are taught that they should NEVER use their sticks as weapons. There are strict rules to prevent this. To see a veteran, professional player do this in a regulation game, and get away with just a minor penalty is beyond the pale! The NHL Discipline Committee, or even Commissioner Bettman himself, should haul Avery's sorry butt into their offices for a **reprimand**, a **substantial fine**, AND a **suspension**. The rule is, to me, so fundamental that its violation merit's the severest of repudiation.

****

As far as the game itself is concerned, I was pleased with the result. For the first time since 1993, the Leafs have opened a season with four straight wins. This game showcased the skills of Phil Kessel, who demonstrated that he learned something from the last game he played. Ron Wilson felt that Phil was staying out for too long on his shifts early in the game, and was trying to do too much himself. So, Wilson benched him for a while. Message delivered. Last night, Kessel responded with a disciplined and skilful display of hockey, and was rewarded by two goals and an assist. Komisarek and MacArthur scored the other Leaf markers.

This young team learned something else last night. They should NEVER take their foot off the throat of an enemy who they are in the process of defeating. They did that in this game, and saw a two-goal advantage disappear. It took one of Kessel's patented wrist shots to secure victory in the overtime period. They could have put the Rangers away when they had a two-man advantage for nearly two minutes, but they got a bit cute trying to pass the puck back and forth in the New York zone, and didn't succeed in getting the puck near the net.

Next up will be the Islanders, on Monday at the ACC. Will last night's lessons be applied? Will the winning trend continue? **STAY TUNED!**

Leafs Angry & Frustrated by Overtime Loss

The Maple Leafs should have won last night's game at the ACC, but they didn't! It was a very entertaining game. Both teams played very well. The paying crowd certainly got their money's worth. Their favourite team remains undefeated in regulation time, but the Leafs' record is no longer perfect. Moulson and Kessel scored for their respective clubs in regulation. John Tavares scored in overtime to gain the win for the Islanders. His goal means that Leaf fans wil nowl just have to be satisfied with 90 percent.

With the passage of time, we'll probably just think of last night as "one of those nights". There were a number of factors that converged, and the end result just didn't favour the home team. On another night, those same factors could just as easily cause the other team to come out on the short end of the stick. There was very little to choose between the two combatants in this match.

Let's think about the "convergence of factors" that I referred to above. What were they? I submit the following opinions:

Factor 1 - Poor Ice Conditions   Factor 2 - Too many Leaf turnovers
Factor 3 - Marginal Officiating

Kris Vertsteeg missed a couple of scoring opportunities that, on a good night, he would have cashed in for sure. After the game, he commented that the puck was bouncing around more than usual, and he just couldn't make the kind of contact that he needed to score. Over time, I have noticed that there have been a number of occasions when players have complained about the ice at the Air Canada Centre. That seems to be a problem in both the Spring and the Fall, and probably has a lot to do with the tricky humidity readings that can occur when the seasons change.

I heard the radio commentators following the game remarking upon the rather large number of Leaf turnovers…more than twenty in the game. That has been a problem which I noticed, particularly in the pre-season. I am optimistic that this flaw in the Leaf game will be corrected as the season unfolds. Even though such was the case last night, it didn't hurt them too badly.

Marginal officiating CAN happen from time to time. Watching a replay of the game this morning, I would have to concur with the paying crowd, who very clearly voiced their displeasure with the officials. There certainly appeared to be several questionable decisions on their part. If the supervising officials agree that the on-ice personnel did not perform to expectations, the referees and linesman will definitely hear about it. NHL officials usually can be counted upon for a high level of efficiency, but they are all human, and from time to time, they have a bad game.

I will look forward to a hometown rebound on Thursday, when the Rangers come to town for their second tilt against the Leafs in this young season.

Sluggish Leafs Outworked by Rangers

Last night, the New York Rangers exacted revenge upon the Maple Leafs for spoiling their home opener in the Big Apple last week. The Broadway Blueshirts scored a well-earned victory over the Leafs, who suffered their first regulation-time loss of the season.

The Leafs were slow out of the gate in this one, and it was clear right from the start that they were not firing on all cylinders. Shots on goal pretty well tell the whole story. The Rangers fired 15 shots at Gustavsson in the first period, scoring two goals off the sticks of Fedotenko and Anisimov. Those goals clearly demoralized the Leafs, and put them in a hole that they could not recover from over the course of the game. Although the Leafs played better during the second period, they were unable to penetrate the Rangers' staunch defence. The visitors blocked an impressive number of Leaf shots as the game progressed, and were very good at protecting Martin Biron, who was playing his first game of the season in the New York net. During the third period, the Leaf effort seemed to tail off again. They only managed 6 shots on goal, but Colby Armstrong scored his first goal as a Leaf, with assists from MacArthur and Grabovski.

There were few Maple Leaf players who could be identified as playing overly well in this match. The two exceptions that I was able to pick out were Luke Schenn and Jonas Gustavsson. Schenn has appeared to improve his game markedly over last season, in which most commentators have said he suffered from the infamous "sophomore jinx". Gustavsson made several very good saves, and therefore kept the Rangers' margin of victory to a single goal.

Ron Wilson and his coaching staff obviously were less than happy with their forward line combinations, and as the game progressed, they began to change some of them around. Tyler Bozak spent a few shifts on the bench, and the so-called "big guns" on the Leaf offence were silenced as the result of the Rangers very efficient defensive play.

Wilson was critical of his forward lines following the game. He pointed out that they appeared unwilling to go to the front of the net, preferring instead to play on the perimeter. Armstrong's goal resulted from one of the few times in the game when the home team DID fire shots from close range. Wilson summed up the game succinctly when he said, "We got what we deserved."

On Saturday, the Leafs play on the road, travelling to Philadelphia, the City of Brotherly Love. The Flyers only have two victories in their first six games, but the Leafs are going to have to pick up their play significantly if they expect to regain their season-opening momentum. A third consecutive loss will not auger well for their team morale, and their fans will begin to wonder and worry all over again.

Back to the Drawing Board

Shades of last year! The Maple Leafs played their absolutely worst game of this young season in Philadelphia last night. After a stellar beginning to the current campaign, they looked ordinary against the Flyers. Actually, they looked worse than ordinary. They played, in the words of Don Cherry, "stupid hockey"!

Over the course of three straight games, the Leafs have plunged from a winning percentage of 100 to a thoroughly mediocre 64. Their goals-per-game has slipped from 4 to 2.8. Inconsistent play has prompted Ron Wilson to tinker with his forward lines in what is beginning to look like an urgency to discover some way of engineering some scoring production.

Things have really started to go south over these last three games. Shots on goal have diminished markedly. The Leafs have been firing shots from the periphery, and many of their shots have been blocked by the opposition. They are not crashing the net the way they were in their four-game winning streak. It seems that they have lost track of the concept of team offence.

Last night's game was an aberration...at least I HOPE it was. Dion Phaneuf had a horrible game, easily his worst as a Leaf. He openly admitted such in his post-game interview. The whole team became dysfunctional early in the contest. At its very beginning, it looked like they came to play. They were putting some pressure on the Flyers, who were stinging as the result of three straight home losses. Gradually though, the Flyers took command, and skated off the ice at the first intermission with a two goal lead, thanks to goals by Richards and Leino.

Phil Kessel scored for the Leafs just as he left the penalty box after serving a dumb "closing the hand on the puck" sentence. Blair Betts restored the Philly two-goal lead. MacArthur then notched his sixth goal of the season to keep Toronto competitive.

Things totally fell apart in the early stages of the third period. Blatant defensive lapses resulted in goals by Hartnell and Briere, and the Leafs folded like a cheap tent. The Leafs were only able to get three shots at Boucher in the Philly net in the final period, and a measly total of fourteen for the whole game. With awful production like that, there is no way that anyone could expect to win a professional hockey game. The trip to Philadelphia was a waste of time.

Wilson and his staff have got to take this team back to the basics...and they haven't got a lot of time to get the job done. The Florida Panthers will visit the ACC on Tuesday evening. Their achievement so far this season is almost equal to the Leafs. They won their game last night over the Islanders, so they will be coming into this match-up on a positive note. The Leafs have some shaping up to do...and not much time to do it!

Leafs Notch Another Win to Sustain Optimism

To be completely honest with you, dear readers, I viewed this game between the Leafs and the Panthers with mixed allegiances. Now, of course, since I have been a Leaf fan since midway through the last century, the majority of my best wishes were directed in favour of Toronto. However, whenever the Florida Panthers face off against the boys in blue and white, I feel obliged to qualify my perspective.

You see, a few years ago, I befriended a very nice couple who had lived in Mississauga for many years. Their names are Rod and Jean. Sadly, Jean is no longer with us. They came to know that I was a long-time hockey fan, and it just so happened that their grandson, named Shawn Matthias, was a very talented hockey player. He had just made the monumental decision to put his talents to the test, and accept an offer to join the Belleville Bulls of the OHL.

Well, to make a long story short, he had a very successful four-year career with the Bulls. He became a major star in the OHL. He represented Canada in the World Junior Championships that were held in the Czech Republic, where he assisted on the goal that won the gold medal.

Shawn was originally drafted into the NHL by the Detroit Red Wings. While still a member of the Bulls, he was traded to the Florida Panthers, in exchange for Todd Bertuzzi. Three years ago, he signed a three-year contract with the Panthers, and he is, today, one of their centres. Unfortunately, he injured his foot in a team practice last Friday, and was unable to play against the Leafs last night.

I am pleased to report though, that the Leafs were able to beat Florida by a final score of 3 to 1. Leaf scorers were Bozak, with his first marker of the season, Orr, who scored a rather controversial winner, and Phil Kessel. Dennis Wideman responded for the Panthers.

Unfortunately, the Leafs sustained a couple of injuries in this match. Colby Armstrong left the game during the first period with a serious hand injury. It will require surgery, and he will miss several weeks while he recovers. Kris Verbeek is also complaining of a sore back, and it is unclear just how many games that he will miss. Luca Caputi has been called up from the Marlies as a replacement for Armstrong.

The Leafs have two more games this month…Thursday in Boston against the Bruins, and Saturday at home with the New York Rangers paying a visit. To this point in the season, I have refrained from making too many evaluative statements. I will venture a brief overview of the team following Saturday's tenth match. These two games will be very tough challenges for this refurbished Maple Leaf club. Good luck, boys!

Tim Thomas Backstops Boston to Leaf Whitewash

The Maple Leafs worked very hard last night, but they were frustrated at every turn. A staunch defence mounted by the hometown Bruins kept them at bay, and that, combined with another reliable effort by goalie Tim Thomas, resulted in a 2 - 0 victory The Boston goals were notched by Bergeron and Seguin.

At first glance, the Leafs played a fairly good game. There was, in fact, very little that one could criticize about their performance. Why, then, did they lose?

Before this game began, the Bruins held an impressive centre-ice ceremony to celebrate the great career of Milt Schmidt. Milt was a former player, coach, and executive of their organization, and one of the most famous NHL players in history. At the conclusion of the presentation, all of the current Bruin players lined up to shake Milt's hand. I was very impressed with their size as they filed past Schmidt, their 94-year-old honouree of the evening's festivities.

Did the Leafs lose to a bigger, stronger team? To help determine the answer to that question, I decided to do a statistical comparison between the two clubs, specifically the forwards and the defenceman. The Leaf forwards average height is 6 feet, three inches…one inch less than the Bruins' 6 feet, four. The average weight of the forwards on both teams is exactly the same, 201 pounds. The Boston defenders are definitely bigger than the Leafs. They average six feet, six inches, over the Toronto average of six feet, three inches. In terms of weight, the Leafs outweigh their opponent Beantowners on average by five pounds (216 - 211) Conclusion…size had little to do with the outcome.

The most significant factor, in fact, turns out to be the number of shots on goal. Boston had 32, while the Leafs could only manage 20. I have a pet theory that a successful, competitive hockey team SHOULD average at least ten shots on goal in each period. Failure to do that is usually a pretty clear indication that the winning team has probably kept the losers to the outside, thereby giving their goalie a pretty clear view of the pucks directed his way. When a team can boast a goalie with the skills of a Tim Thomas, that style of play will result in a goodly number of wins.

The Leafs will have to do better on Saturday night. The New York Rangers will pay another visit to the Air Canada Centre. It will be the tenth game of the season for the Leafs. In my mind, this is a must-win game for the boys in blue and white. Once this match is in the record book, I am going to venture my first evaluation of this year's club. I will do my best to be positive, but I rather suspect that this first critical month of the campaign will reveal some aspects of team play, and some individual efforts, that will require some improvements and/or refinements in the future.

A good result on "Hockey Night in Canada" will be a reasonably clear indicator of what we can expect from our Maple Leafs as the current season Unfolds

Hands of Stone

My rather unusual title today pretty well sums up the reason for a very disappointing performance by the Maple Leafs at the Air Canada Centre last night. The Rangers had no business winning this game…but they did! They were a tired club coming into this match. This was the third game in four nights for them, and they were tired almost to the point of exhaustion. Being professionals however, they entered the ACC knowing full well that the vagaries of the NHL schedule were totally out of their control. They would just "suck things up" and do the best they could.

And they did!   And they went home tired but happy with a very fortuitous victory. The Leafs unleashed a tremendous barrage of shots on the visiting club. They fired 36 shots on Hendrik Lundqvist in the New York net, and many more than that in the Ranger zone which were blocked by courageous players in defence of their territory. A slick backhander by Brian Boyle eluded Giguere for the first New York goal. Then, in the second period Ryan Callahan was awarded a penalty shot, and he made no mistake.

The Leafs, on the other side of the puck, couldn't find the net with a search party. Just yesterday, I told you about my theory concerning shots on goal. I related that shots on goal USUALLY help determine a positive outcome in a hockey game. However, we witnessed last night the reality that such is NOT always the case. The infamous Gods of Hockey sometimes intervene, as I believe they did in this contest. They clearly worked against the Leafs. The home team fired a huge number of shots at the Rangers, but they were all blanks. For the second consecutive game, the opposing goalie saw every vulcanized incoming missile clearly, and stoned the Leafs cold.

Who can explain such a one-sided attack coming up empty?

Who can explain why FIVE Maple Leaf players (Schenn, Komisarek, Orr, Kessel, and Grabovsky) had ZERO shots on goal during the entire game? These players averaged sixteen minutes of ice time apiece.

Who can explain why FIVE other Leaf players (Phaneuf, Kaberle, Beauchemin, Caputi, and Bozak) could fire 26 shots on the opposing net **WITHOUT A SINGLE GOAL?**

Last night's game against the Rangers was hanging there like a nice, ripe, shiny apple in an orchard, just waiting to be picked by a hungry Maple Leaf hockey club. Unfortunately, **the Leafs picked the wrong apple …the one with a big, juicy worm inside it!**

Rats!

Evaluation # 1 - The First Month

Where do we stand? The month of October has ended. The Leafs have played ten games. Today would seem to be a natural occasion to pause and take stock of where this team stands in relation to others in the NHL after a month of play.

The Maple Leafs currently possess 11 points. In the overall league standings, that places them 19th in a league of 30 teams. The San Jose Sharks and the New York Rangers also have 11 points.

In the Eastern Conference, Toronto is in 9th place, tied with the Rangers among the 15 teams.

In the Northeast Division, Toronto stands 3rd among the 5 teams

At the end of October, one year ago, the Leafs had 4 points out of a possible 24...which had them with a winning percentage of 16%. This year, at the same juncture, the Leafs' winning percentage stands at 56%.

In summary, The Toronto Maple Leafs are hovering around the middle of the pack, with a significantly improved standing over last year's club.

****

The Leafs have played ten games in October. By sheer coincidence, they will also play ten games in November. **THEY WILL HAVE TO DO BETTER THIS MONTH!**

Elsewhere in this work, I have stated that the ONLY objective of the Maple Leaf franchise this season is that of **making the playoffs** If that objective is to be achieved, the Leafs MUST wind up their regular season with a standing that is well above the "middle of the pack". Let's do the math.

The current level of 56%, if projected over the full schedule's total possible points would give the team 92 points. That total would have been enough to qualify them for the playoffs in the Eastern Conference last year...but NOT in the Western Conference. **Therefore, I believe that the Leafs should strive for at least a 65% winning percentage this year.**

NOTHING LESS SHOULD BE ACCEPTABLE!

****

In making evaluations throughout my career as an educator, I always tried my best to focus on the POSITIVE aspects of whatever or whoever I was formulating my opinions about. I will try to do the same here.

- This year's team is definitely better than was the case this year…and I believe that it has the potential to improve upon their encouraging start to the season.

- Goaltending has been reliable to this point in time. Giguere has played in seven games… Gustavsson in three. Giguere's mentoring of his younger colleague appears to be going well. Both goalies have provided solid play in the Leaf net throughout all ten games played to date.

- The Defence gets mixed reviews at this time. They have provided their goalies with an adequate degree of protection, and therefore the Leafs have been in contention MOST of the time. In terms of scoring, the record is much less impressive. Defenders have only recorded TWO goals…one by Beauchemin, and one by Komisarek. To me, that represents inadequate support, and will need to improve as the season progresses. Luke Schenn is impressing me with his style of play so far this year. Dion Phaneuf, from time to time, appears to be struggling with his new role as Leaf Captain. Kaberle, Komisarek, and Beauchemin are capable of stronger performances.

- The forwards are sputtering in terms of production. Only Kessel and MacArthur have impressed me at all. All of the remainder of the forwards have performed below expectations. In spite of having experimented with several combinations, Ron Wilson and his staff have been frustrated at every turn. Goals per game have tailed off to a very poor 2.3, and that sort of production will not provide the power needed to garner a spot in post-season play. There will need to be a marked improvement up front in the month of November.

****

In summary, the Leafs are off to a reasonably good start. Although they have experienced a bit of frustration in recent games, I believe that they have the capability of getting back into a positive mind set, and therefore can expect a greater degree of success. The end of November will see the club reach the quarter point of the schedule, and we will have a clearer picture of its potential at that time.

Trouble Strikes Without Mercy

I went to bed last night feeling a deep sense of foreboding gloom. The Leaf loss to the Ottawa Senators was the first reason for my concern.

The second was the uncertainty that I still feel as I write this about the injury sustained by Captain Dion Phaneuf. Early in the second period of this game, he went hard into the corner with an Ottawa player. It was instantly apparent that Dion was hurt. He appeared to be in significant pain. Initial speculation revolved around whether the injury involved his left knee or ankle. We now know that he sustained a deep cut, and was taken by ambulance to a hospital to make sure that he was properly diagnosed and treated. We will find out later today just how long the team will be without Phaneuf in the line-up.

Thirdly, I am becoming increasingly concerned about the plummeting offensive production of the team. After playing four games, the Leafs were averaging 4 goals per game. They are now, after their 11th game, barely managing 2 goals per game. As I watched the initial stages of this match, I was struck by the fact that NOBODY on the team was having any luck around the opposing net. Not a single player was showing any signs of breaking out of the horrendous scoring slump that has seen the team shut out for the past two and two-thirds games. Unless this team can restore their earlier rate of goal production, they cannot hope to remain competitive in the league.

The Leafs finally broke their scoring drought in the third period, when Kulemin and MacArthur were credited with goals. It was too little, too late though. I am astonished that there have not been more players able to put some pucks in the net. Kessel and MacArthur are the only players who can claim any consistency as far as scoring is concerned. These two guys cannot be expected to carry the club. Everyone else…and I mean EVERYONE, has got to step up and get this club rolling again.

The Leafs have to start their reversal of fortune tonight, as they take on the Washington Capitals in USA's capital city. Of course, in this one they will face the "Great 8"…Alex Ovechkin. We all know just how fierce a competitor he can be. If he gets on a roll, he can single-handedly tear a team to shreds. This year's Capitals are still stinging from their early departure from last spring's playoffs, and they are determined to reclaim the high spot in the standings that they had last season.

The Washington Capitals have won 7 of their first 11 games. They will give the Leafs everything that they can handle tonight. With Dion Phaneuf sidelined, the Leafs will need all hands on deck in order to have any chance at all to claim a victory.

Leafs Lose a Thriller Via Shootout

"Bittersweet" is probably a good word to use when describing the Leafs' effort in Washington, D.C. last night. While they lost the extra point to the Caps in the shootout, the club fought back from a two-goal deficit to claim one point at the end of a 4 - 4 regulation time tie.

I looked upon this game as somewhat of a turning point for the Leafs…for a couple of very important reasons. First of all, this was the first game of the season that they would be without their Captain. The injury that Dion Phaneuf suffered the other night against the Senators was far more serious than was first apparent. He was cut very deeply on the back of his left thigh, and required surgery to repair a nick on his medial collateral ligament, as well as stitches to muscle and flesh. He will be lost to the team for at least four weeks, and possibly more.

There is now a leadership void that MUST be fulfilled by someone. It will be interesting to see just who…if anyone…will step forward in an attempt to keep the team's tenuous forward momentum going in the right direction.

I also felt that this game had considerable importance in the team's efforts to break out of their recent scoring slump. The Leafs appeared to be in the grips of a downward spiral that seemed to be sucking the good air out of the ACC of late. For the past couple of games, the crowds had been silenced, because there was very little going on to excite them The "boo-birds" had even revealed a degree of displeasure.

The first period gave us a glimmer of what was to come. Nikolai Kulemin scored a goal, marking the first time in a few games in which the Leafs scored first. The second period took the wind out of our sails because Green, Chimera, and Fleischmann put the Capitals ahead by two.

The Leafs came out flying to start the third period. Before the eight minute mark, goals by Brown, Versteeg, and Bozak had the score tilt in favour of the visitors. Alas, a final goal from the stick of Alexander Semin tied the game at 4 - 4. The Leafs then hung on for the single point. A five-minute overtime session solved nothing. In the shootout, Toronto was unable to score, and Semin was credited with the winner for the Caps.

I saw a bit of a lesson for the Leafs during the early part of the third period last night. The Leafs came out of their dressing room with a vengeance. They accelerated their pace, and Ron Wilson gave more ice time to players who showed that they were firing on all cylinders. That is the way that the Leafs are going to have to play in order to have success. They are going to have to rely on their speed and size to overpower their opponents. Their aggression level, over the course of the next few games, will have to be set on "HIGH"! Players who can't do that will have to "ride the pine" until they get it.

November 6, 2010

Establishing a Formula for Success

The Leafs need a winning formula!

Ever since watching the way that the Toronto Maple Leafs came back to overcome a two goal lead against the Washington Capitals the other night, I have been thinking about that.

They need to have a formula for all of them to visualize before every game. It must be simple and direct. It has to be something that every player, **TO A MAN**, can buy into. Then, with that formula burned into their psyche, **they have to go out and EXECUTE IT!**

Let's make a list of some of the attributes of this year's team:
> They are big. The average weight of the Leaf players is 208 pounds.
> They are young. The average age of the team is 26.7.
> They have considerable capacity for speed

Those three realities alone suggest to me that the Leafs could be nearing the peak of their potential as a team. They may be a year…perhaps two away from forming a championship club, but <u>they are close</u>.

I would suggest that there is one attribute that is, for the present time at least, a bit lacking in the overall makeup of this group of aspiring professional hockey players, and that quality is… **UNBRIDLED PASSION!**

Think of Stamkos. Think of Ovechkin. Think of Crosby. Think of the Sedin twins. Think of Gretzky. Think of Orr. Think of Esposito. The list goes on and on. Now, of course I realize that the Leafs cannot ALL perform at the emotional and artistic levels of these superstars, but why can't the Leafs have just two or three? Right now, we have Kessel as a strong possibility to fulfill a similar role. I submit that there can, and should be a couple of others who COULD step up to the challenge

<u>SIZE</u> + <u>YOUTH</u> + <u>SPEED</u> + <u>PASSION</u> = SUCCESS

That sounds like a formula that could work for the boys in blue and white! It isn't rocket science! It's not hard to memorize. The coaches could paint it on the locker room wall, if they wanted. If the formula can be applied in MOST of the games that they play…**IT COULD WORK!**

WOULDN'T THAT BE A TREAT FOR ALL OF US?

An Inexcusable Loss

Thirteen seconds and two Buffalo Sabres' shots are all that separated the Leafs from two points last night. As the red light signaled the winning goal for the visitors, "Hockey Canada" showed GM Brian Burke wheeling away from his perch high above the ACC ice, heading for the door. I rather suspect that the air was blue with expletives.

I am going to lay the blame for this disappointing loss exactly where I think it belongs… squarely on the shoulders of Ron Wilson and the coaching staff. The Leafs were not ready for the Buffalo Sabres last night. They were ripe for the picking. Buffalo had played a game the previous night. They were tired. Ryan Miller, their superb front line goalie, was sitting this game out due to an injury. In his stead, the Sabres were playing a diminutive replacement whom the Leafs had never faced before. When one of the Buffalo players first encountered Enroth, he allegedly said, "This is our goalie? Where's the other half?" Going into last night's game, the Sabres were tied for LAST PLACE in the league.

It was the responsibility of the Toronto coaching staff to make the Leaf players fully aware of all these things about their opponent. The home team should have come out of the gate with all guns blazing, and crushed their opponent into submission in the first period. They didn't! Their effort was half-hearted at best. The game was moribund in nature! There were not enough shots directed at the Buffalo net.. Leaf passing was inept, and nobody was causing any problems in front of the enemy net. Yesterday, I wrote about the need for this team to start playing with some PASSION…some P*** and Vinegar! That simply isn't happening.

And then, there was the final minute of the game. WHY, in the name of the gods of hockey, was the FOURTH line on the ice when the Sabres had pulled their goalie to enable a sixth attacker to enter the play? Whose decision was that? I'll give you three guesses, and the first two don't count.

This Leaf team is in trouble, dammit! The centres aren't playing worth diddley squat! They have registered only 5 goals in 13 games! Unacceptable! Hanson and Mitchell combined have only a single point! Unacceptable! Versteeg has only five points thus far. Two or three other forwards are statistically almost invisible. Without some rather dramatic improvements in the near future, this team is NOT going to qualify for the post-season…AGAIN!

UNACCEPTABLE!!!!!

This week, the Leafs play Tampa Bay, Florida, and Vancouver. It's high time to get the lead out of their butts, and get back into contention.

And that statement includes the coaching staff!

Adrift in the NHL

This morning, off the western coast of Mexico and the USA a huge cruise ship loaded with vacationers drifts aimlessly, waiting until tugboats arrive tomorrow to tow it into port. Apparently there was a fire in the engine room, and the vessel's propulsion system was disabled, leaving the ship adrift at sea.

Sound familiar?

As I watched the Leaf/Lightning game on television last night, I saw a team adrift in the NHL. The Maple Leafs had zero propulsion. Although there were three players wearing the "A" in the absence of their injured leader, there was zero leadership being exercised by anyone. If there were orders or instructions being issued by the coaching staff, there was zero response from the skaters on the ice.

The other day, I used the word "unacceptable" repeatedly to describe the way the Maple Leafs are playing over the past few games. This morning, the headline on the Toronto Star's sports page blares that same word. This time, it is uttered as a quote of Jean Sebastien Giguere, the team's veteran goalie. Victimized by the lacklustre effort in front of him, he publicly scolded the young, listless group of team-mates who did little to get the club out of the doldrums in which they are aimlessly drifting.

Tonight, I will watch again, as our 46.4 percent Leafs play the 42 percent Florida Panthers. Sounds exciting, doesn't it?

Brian Burke, back in Toronto attending a meeting of the League's General Managers, must be going nuts as he watches his team falling apart in front of his eyes. I can only imagine some of the questions going through his mind. Let me suggest what some of them may be:

- I am paying in excess of $21 million dollars to the defencemen on my team. How come the best blue line player is the one who is earning less than a million? (Schenn - $875,000)
- Where in the devil are my centre men? They are invisible. Seventeen points in fourteen games is ridiculous in terms of offensive production.
- Kulemin and MacArthur are the only left-wingers showing effort and ability up front. Sjostrom (1 point) and Caputi (zero) are barely on the radar.
- Where in the world has Kessel been lately? He hasn't scored a single point in **SIX STRAIGHT GAMES! This guy is my Superstar???**

In the words of a well-known TSN hockey commentator, "This team is in a world of hurt!"

When will it end?

Leafs in Full-Blown Crisis Mode

Earlier in this work, I have told you that although I am a faithful Leaf fan, I also have a personal interest in the Florida Panthers. The focus of that interest is one of their young centres, named Shawn Matthias. Shawn had a very good game against the Leafs last night, scoring a goal and adding an assist. He now has three goals and three assists on the season. He and the Panthers skated off with a well-deserved win.

The Leafs, on the other hand, had yet another inept effort, and consequently racked up their seventh consecutive loss. Grabovski finally scored for the Leafs, but his goal came late in the third period…too little, too late…AGAIN!

Most fans would agree that this team is now immersed in a full blown crisis. As I listened to the post-game radio program following last night's contest, I realized that everyone who called in to that show reflected that reality through their comments. The frustration being experienced by this team is clearly apparent in their play, and there is no evidence that any kind of turnaround is imminent. With the Vancouver Canucks visiting the ACC on Saturday night, visions of a bloodbath on Bay Street are flashing before my eyes.

I don't have any answers or solutions to escape this current dilemma. The only thing that I can do is offer some suggestions that may be worthy of consideration. So, here goes:

1. Brian Burke is the head honcho of the Leafs. He must take command. He should sit down with Dave Nonis and anyone else in top management positions to set a plan for a turnaround…**NOW!**

2. Burke and the management team must decide whether or not there needs to be a coaching change. Have these players quit on Ron Wilson and his staff? Is there a "generation gap" between the players and the coaches that is leading to relationship and communication issues? Are there any player "attitudes" that may be poisoning the atmosphere among the ranks of the players? Players and coaches MUST be on the same page. If such is not the case, either a coach, or coaches must be changed, or any offending player must be dealt with by the manager, **MR. BURKE.**

3. On last night's telecast the following words were uttered by one of the commentators, "The Leafs have ZERO centres right now." I believe that management should:
> * keep Mikhail Grabovski
> * recall Mike Zigomanis from the Marlies
> * keep the ONE most promising player of Hanson, Bozak, Mitchell, or Brent

> * Use some cap money for acquisition of a centre from the NHL list of Unrestricted Free Agents

* Avoid recalling Nazem Kadri until at least Game # 41. (Mid-season)

Grabovski has 9 points. He is working hard. Zigomanis is doing well with the Marlies, and would probably respond positively to a promotion to the big club. Management can probably decide which of the four centres I've mentioned has the greatest future potential. Keep that one, and demote the rest. Then, spend a few bucks and sign one from the UFA list.. **Recalling Kadri should be a last resort.**

That done, let those four players know that it is up to them to take charge of increasing offensive production, and turn them loose to get the job done.

4. As far as the wingers are concerned, I would suggest that a degree of patience be observed until the issue of the centres gets settled. It seems reasonable to make a major attempt to resolve one or two of the most critical issues, rather than get into a wholesale team shake-up. That sort of measure would probably not be practical in mid-season anyway.

I am sure that every true Maple Leaf fan is very, very worried about the current mess in which this team finds itself. I am also certain that the players themselves are eager to have things sorted out and remedied.

One fact is very clear to me, and I am certain that Brian Burke is equally cognizant of the same thing. The Maple Leaf team is in "critical condition". There are FIVE games left until the first quarter of the regular season is complete. It is my feeling that the Leafs MUST reach the 22 point level by then.. If they don't, the likelihood of reaching the post-season will become doubtful, at best.

MISSING THE PLAYOFFS THIS SEASON IS NOT AN OPTION. THERE IS STILL TIME TO RIGHT THE SHIP AND GET THINGS BACK ON COURSE.

HOWEVER…TIME IS RUNNING OUT!

MR. BURKE……….THE BALL IS IN YOUR COURT!

Giguere Miscue Costly to Leafs

Those faceless, nameless, mystical hockey gods are still working against the Maple Leafs as they continued their agonizing plunge to the depths of the NHL standings last night. This time, they came back to bite goalie J.S. Giguere on the bum. Earlier this week, he spoke critically of the work ethic of the players in front of him. Last night, a shot fired at him from more than forty feet out slipped between his legs, and that shot from the stick of Mason Raymond proved to be the winner for the visiting Canucks.

Up to that point in the third period, it had been a very interesting game. The match was tied 3 - 3. Vancouver goals had been scored by Daniel Sedin and Ryan Kessler (2), and the Leafs had notched markers by Kessel, Sjostrom, and Grabovski. After Raymond's winner, the Leafs pulled Giguere for an extra attacker, but that measure backfired when Hamhuis fired the clincher into an empty net.

So, the slide continues. With four games remaining until the Leafs reach the quarter pole, those four games must ALL be considered as MUST-WINS. If this team fails to earn at least twenty points by the end of their twentieth game, they will have dug themselves into a hole that will be almost as bad as last year's, and it will be virtually impossible to regain any hope of post-season play.

Last night marked the return to the big league of Nazem Kadri. Although I wrote just a few days ago that his recall should have been regarded as a Last resort, the Leaf braintrust thought otherwise, and he is now a Leaf. Whether or not he stays with the big club for the remainder of the season will depend upon his ability to prove his effectiveness as an NHL performer. I wish him all the best.

Keith Aulie was also recalled from the Marlies to bolster the Leaf defence. He played a very good game, and it was nice to see his parents in attendance to support him.

I am a trifle concerned about the recent play of Phil Kessel, and I am beginning to perceive rumblings of criticism from the media. He did score a goal last night, but I believe that it is safe to say he is not playing as aggressively, or with the same skill as he has shown in the past. Naturally, in Toronto he is squarely under the microscope. If his performance cannot remain at a level that meets the expectations placed upon him following his acquisition from Boston, the wrath of the Leaf Nation will know no bounds. He will suffer the consequences, and so will Brian Burke.

Let's not have any illusions here, folks. The Leafs are up to their butts in a major crisis. Although there may have been a glimmer of hope last night, they still surrendered both points that were there for the taking. These next four games are crucial beyond belief!

A Weird End to a Losing Streak

I watched the first period of the Leaf - Predators game last night hardly able to believe my eyes. I was almost physically ill as the Leafs played as if they were bent on self-destruction. I cannot even imagine what kind of thoughts were coursing through the minds of Ron Wilson and his coaching staff. An outburst of goals by Dumont, Tootoo, and Erat put the Leafs down by a score of 3 - 0, and they were turning the puck over to the visiting team time after time. The hometown crowd was booing the Leafs at the top of their lungs. It was downright UGLY.

Finally, near the end of the period, Luke Schenn scored, and the Leafs skated to their dressing room on a bit of a promising note.

It looked like that promise was short-lived when Marcel Goc stripped the puck from Brett Lebda, and scored the fourth Nashville goal on Giguere. Then, the weirdest and almost unimaginable series of events took place. One after another, the Predators were assessed a string of penalties, and the Leafs scored FOUR CONSECUTIVE POWER-PLAY GOALS. By the end of the middle frame, they were in the lead. They had turned the entire game around from front to back. Everyone, including myself, was astonished!

I have no idea which member of the coaching staff made the decision to try Kris Versteeg on the point in power play situations, but it looked like a stroke of genius. He played what was probably his best game as a Leaf, and started the team's recovery by scoring two goals. Two others were added by Grabovski and Kulemin to give the Leafs the lead.

There was no scoring in the third. Nashville tried hard to regain the lead that they had lost. They fired 14 shots at the Leaf net, but were unsuccessful. I'm sure that they attributed this loss to the fact that they did not play a disciplined game for the full sixty minutes.

J. S. Giguere surprised almost everyone partway through the third period when he skated over to the Leaf bench and informed Ron Wilson that he had sustained a groin injury. Jonas Gustavsson entered the game, and completed it even though Giguere did return to the bench. We now know that he has suffered a groin pull, and will miss the next few games. Jamie Reimer has been called up from the Marlies to back up Gustavsson, who was named third star of this game on the basis of six critical saves in relief of "Jiggy".

Last night's game was just the first of a series of must-win situations. The next three games fall into that same category. New Jersey comes in on Thursday, and the Leafs absolutely MUST win that contest. If they lose, we're back to "square one". The team has no choice but to build upon the triumph that they pulled off against the Preds.

Two in a Row …AND THEY'RE WINS!!!

I feel a little less tense this morning … just a little, though. Having watched the Leafs stagger and stumble through their first eighteen games, I am doing my best to retain a reasonably objective stance as I chronicle their journey through the regular NHL schedule. Their latest two performances have definitely eased the anguish that was beginning to creep over me.

Last night, the boys in blue and white came through with their second win in as many games. They put up a very sound and solid effort against the New Jersey Devils, who are also struggling through a frustrating start to their season. Life in the swamp has not been good for the Devils this year. They have won only FIVE games thus far, while dropping TWELVE. In spite of boasting arguably the best goalie in NHL history (Martin Brodeur) and one of the most prolific scorers in the league (Ilya Kovalchuk), the Devils are not playing well at all. Their only scorer last night was Danius Zubrus, and Brodeur aggravated an injury, excusing himself from the match at the end of the second period.

The hometown boys, however, rose to the challenge and performed impressively. In the net, Jonas Gustavsson stopped 29 of the 30 shots fired at him as he played the first of several games in which he will appear in relief of the injured J. S. Giguere.

The defence corps also played a solid game. Both Komisarek and Kaberle picked up assists during the course of their evening's work.

Up front and on the attack there were some very promising signs that this is indeed a better team than their current record shows. Clarke MacArthur picked up another assist, and continued his stalwart play as a Leaf. Phil Kessel scored his ninth goal, and is starting to get his name recorded on the score sheet with greater frequency than he did just a few games ago. All eyes are watching young Nazem Kadri, who picked up his second and third assists in his 3rd game since being recalled by the Leafs. Many people, myself included, felt that he should have spent more time with the Marlies, but he has performed very well thus far, and could prove himself as a legitimate major-leaguer as the season goes on.

The Leafs will finish the first quarter of the season with games against Montreal, on Saturday, and the Dallas Stars on Monday. Playing in the Bell Centre tomorrow evening will be a huge challenge. The Habs have gotten off to a good start, but they are stinging a bit this morning after losing 3 - 0 to the Predators last night. Monday's opponent, the Stars, will enter that game boasting a decent start to their season, too.

The Leafs cannot let up in the least. Four more points would re-establish them as contenders as they enter the second quarter of league play.

Patrick (Pat) Burns
April 4, 1952 - November 19, 2010

The world of hockey today mourns the passing of Pat Burns, one of the most colourful and respected men to ever grace the arenas and offices of the National Hockey League. Pat died yesterday at the age of 58, following a long battle with cancer.

Born in Montreal, Quebec, Pat rose to fame as a head coach in the NHL beginning in 1988 with the Montreal Canadiens. (1988 to 1992). After being dismissed from the Canadiens, he was hired by the Toronto Maple Leafs. (1992 - 1996). His coaching career continued with the Boston Bruins (1997 - 2001), and concluded with the New Jersey Devils (2002 - 2005). In total, he coached in the NHL for 14 seasons.

He coached the New Jersey Devils to the Stanley Cup in 2003.

He was named the Jack Adams Award winner as NHL Coach of the Year:
>   **in 1989, with the Canadiens,**
>   **in 1993, with the Leafs,   and**
>   **in 1998, with the Bruins.**

After being diagnosed with colon cancer in 2004, he accepted the position of special assignment coach with the Devils, a position which he held until his passing. He defeated colon cancer and liver cancer, but when the disease attacked his lungs, he made the decision not to undergo treatment, because the doctors informed him that the disease was terminal. Pat died in Sherbrooke yesterday in hospice care.

In his memory, the Pat Burns Arena is under construction in Stanstead, Quebec, and will be completed in 2011. Pat, himself, presided at the ground-breaking ceremony.

****

Earlier this year, the selection committee was petitioned to admit Pat Burns into the Hockey Hall of Fame, while he was still alive. Sadly, that did not happen, and it is widely felt that this decision will be forever regarded as a regrettable mistake.

Pat Burns belongs in the Hall of Fame...I am certain of that!

As a coach of four NHL teams, his reputation, briefly outlined above, is impeccable. He was skilled. He was genuinely admired, even loved by a huge number of the players who skated for him. As this is written, tributes are flooding media outlets as the news spreads about our loss. Burns was not only known for his prowess behind the bench, but by his larger than life personality, but by his love of the game itself, and the loyalty and devotion that he always demonstrated to the organizations that employed him throughout his career.

Have you ever visited a Hall of Fame?

I am thrilled to be able to say that I have visited TWO such places. I have travelled to the Baseball Hall of Fame in Cooperstown, New York, and the Hockey Hall of Fame in downtown Toronto.

It is difficult to describe the feeling that one gets when you are in the actual halls in both Toronto and Cooperstown, where the plaques and bronze replications of the members are displayed. It is akin to being in a cathedral. The atmosphere is quiet, and one is able to read and ponder the achievements recorded there. I can still **vividly** remember my visits to BOTH Halls of Fame. They were two of the most memorable events of my life.

Pat Burns should have been enrolled in the Hockey Hall of Fame just a couple of weeks ago. He probably would not have been able to attend the induction ceremony, but he would have known that he had reached the very pinnacle of his life's work. He would have been able to feel the love that the hockey world would have directed to him as he lay dying.

In the future, I genuinely hope that the selection committee of the Hockey Hall of Fame deliberates about this situation. In my view, TWO things should happen in 2011.

 * **A "special circumstance" consideration should be instituted that would allow induction of deserving candidates who are either on their deathbeds, or have been tragically taken from us by circumstances beyond anyone's control.**

 * **<u>Pat Burns should be inducted, posthumously, without any further delay!</u>**

Leafs Lose Barnburner to Habs

Each year, for the past several years, the Maple Leaf organization supports an event that has proven to be a wonderful way of acknowledging the contributions of the players' dads to their careers. They select a road game, and invite all the fathers to accompany their sons on the trip. It is a wonderful gesture on the part of the team, and this year's trip to Montreal, held this weekend, was enjoyed by one and all. I hope that, somewhere along the line, their MOTHERS are feted, as well.

The only shadow cast upon this occasion was the 2 0 loss suffered by the Maple Leafs at the hands of their arch-enemy Canadiens.

The boys can hold their heads up high, though. The solid effort was there. They fired 30 shots against Carey Price in the Montreal net, but he stoned them completely with another one of his superb performances. He made the two goals scored by Halpern and Cammalleri stand up for the win. At the other end of the rink, Jonas Gustavsson put on another one of his stellar efforts in a losing cause.

Although I was hoping that the Leafs might be able to get at least one point in the Montreal game, I also feared the worst. After all, the Habs came into this one having won an even dozen of their previous games. They occupied first place in the Northeast Division, and the Leafs were last. It is clear that, at the present time, Montreal has a much better team. In addition to that reality, Montreal goaltender Carey Price has been playing brilliantly, thus giving the skaters all kinds of confidence that he can be depended upon as their last line of defence.

I do, however, expect that the Leafs will win tomorrow evening's contest against the Dallas Stars. It will be their 20th game, a genuine milestone within the current season. The Leafs badly need the two points that are there for the taking. If they are successful, they will be able to enter the second quarter with a reasonable expectation of true respectability by the end of the calendar year. It will not be easy, though. The Stars, even though they are last in their division, still have a better record than Toronto.

Following tomorrow evening's critical game, I will give you my first extensive evaluation of the Leafs as they complete the first quarter of the regular season schedule. Their single objective remains…that of qualifying for post-season play. In order to achieve that goal, team chemistry and the skills of the game will have to merge with harmony. If that cannot happen, the franchise will remain cloaked in mediocrity, and the Burke management team cannot afford to let that happen.

Leafs Outshine the Stars

The Toronto Maple Leafs completed the first quarter of their schedule last night with a convincing 4 - 1 win over the Dallas Stars. I was delighted that the home town won the game. As you know, I regarded this match to be a "must-win", and my evaluation of the first quarter will clearly illustrate just why I held that view.

I must say that I was a little bit puzzled at the end of the first period. The Leafs went to their dressing room with a one-goal lead, courtesy of Nik Kulemin's deflection of a Luke Schenn point shot. The television commentators were expressing satisfaction with the way the game was going. All seemed well with the world...to them. At the time, I was NOT as pleased with what I was seeing. I thought that the pace of the game was sluggish. I did not see a whole lot of jump to the Leaf game. They were not skating as fast, or with aas much energy as they had displayed all through the game on Saturday night against Montreal. The score was okay, but I was wishing that the Leafs would pick up the pace a bit, and work harder to produce more offence. Why, I wondered, was MY opinion so different than what the broadcasters were describing?

I was watching the game live on a very small television screen at my dialysis station in the Renal Ward at Credit Valley Hospital in Mississauga. By the time I got home, the game was being replayed on Leafs TV, and my home television set is a 37" wide-screen, high definition model. It struck me then that the difference in perspective produced by the bigger screen gives one a very much clearer impression of the action on the ice. Last night convinced me that a hockey game can create divergent opinions among viewers, dependent upon their individual point of view.

Anyway, the Leafs went on and played the next two periods with enough energy and skill to wrap up the win. Kulemin got another goal, with Tyler Bozak and Kris Versteeg counting two more. Brad Richards was the only Dallas player to get a puck past Leaf goalie Jonas Gustavsson, who played a very strong game. Another very impressive effort came from Mikhail Grabovski. Kris Versteeg is starting to look very comfortable on his new team, and Luke Schenn is REALLY cementing his rightful place as one of the strongest and most effective Leaf defencemen. There was a bit of a sidelight n last night's game when Ron Wilson, displeased with a lack of defensive effort on the part of Phil Kessel, benched his star left-winger for most of the second period. Wilson's message was clearly "play the game both ways...or SIT DOWN". I think that Phil got the message.

So, dear readers, here we are. Twenty games down...sixty-two to go! In the next pages, I will provide you with my clear assessments and opinions of where the team sits, and where we have to get to, and what has to happen in order to achieve success. We have already experienced some UPS and some DOWNS. There will undoubtedly be more of both as the journey unfolds. Hang onto your hats!

Evaluation - The Leafs at the Quarter Pole

My purpose today is to take a detailed look at the 2010 -2011 Toronto Maple Leaf hockey team, and assess their progress towards their stated goal of making the playoffs in the Spring of the next calendar year.

I will examine the club position by position, give you some data to consider, and then present a few of my personal observations and conclusions. In the end, I hope to set the stage for the second quarter of the schedule, and beyond.

Goaltenders

To this point in the season, both Jean Sebastien Giguere and Jonas Gustavsson have shared time tending the nets for the Leafs. Giguere has, to this point, been the team's primary goaltender. Here are some salient statistics about the goalies.

	Giguere	Gustavsson
Game Appearances	12	9
Shots Against	316	244
Goals Against	33	19
Goals Against Average	2.78	2.30
Save Percentage	.895	.922

Both goalies are obviously performing reasonably well. Giguere, the senior of the two players, is acting as a mentor to the younger Gustavsson, and is doing so effectively. Gustavsson accepts this relationship graciously. He shows on a daily basis that he is a "team player". He is always ready to step in when needed, and is anxious to perform to the best of his ability. Right now, the Leafs have solid, capable goaltending.

Defence

The Leaf defence has allowed 65 goals to be scored against the team in the first quarter. Only 7 teams have allowed more goals. 22 have allowed fewer. These figures show clearly that the Leaf defence needs to improve their work a bit, They should be able to move more towards "the centre of the pack".

To date, the Leafs have employed the services of 9 defencemen patrolling the blue line. Their contributions to the offence is recorded as follows:

Goals - 3   Assists   - 29   **Total Points - 32**

In my view, this contribution to the team's attack is **<u>INADEQUATE</u>**. I expect more offensive support from the back end. This aspect of the game will have to improve if the club is to move up in the standings.

Assessing the defence on an individual basis, Here are the stats:

	Goals	Assists	Points
Beauchemin	1	4	5
Gunnarson	0	1	1
Kaberle	0	10	10
Komisarek	1	5	6
Phaneuf (Injured)	0	4	4
Lebda	0	0	0
Schenn	1	5	6
Aulie	0	0	0
Holzer	0	0	0
TOTALS	**3**	**29**	**32**

To summarize, I offer the following assessments and/or observations:

Beauchemin and Kaberle should be doing better, considering that both are veterans. They should use their ability to shoot more from the point than they are doing so far. They could so a lot more to control the play by "quarterbacking" from the back end. They are capable of much better offensive production.

Komisarek is providing solid, but unspectacular work on defence. I like his positive attitude and demeanor.

Luke Schenn has been, to me, the most impressive performer as a defender.

I expect that Phaneuf's leadership skills will emerge more strongly when he returns to play following his serious leg injury. His presence will be critical as the season moves along.

The remainder of the defensive corps are serving as good, journeyman-type players. Most are young, and should always be trying to improve their game.

Forwards

Altogether, the Toronto Maple Leafs have scored a total of 47 goals in their first 20 games. That is one of the lowest totals in the entire NHL. Only three teams have scored fewer than they have. With the defence accounting for 3 goals, the forwards have scored the other 44. It is clear that the Leaf front line production is currently quite low.

I would also point out here that, although each forward player is evaluated at a specific position, my readers undoubtedly understand that several may have played at other positions at the discretion of the coaching staff.

Centres

The following chart illustrates statistics for the seven players who have played the centre position for the Leafs through their first twenty games.

	Goals	Assists	Points
Grabovski	5	11	16
Bozak	3	3	6
Hanson	0	0	0
Kadri	0	4	4
Mitchell	0	1	1
Brent	2	0	2
Zigomanis	0	1	1
TOTALS	**10**	**20**	**30**

These figures convincingly show that the Leafs have an on-going concern with this position. Grabovski is certainly off to a great start, and can be counted upon to try his hardest every time out. Bozak and Kadri are both youngsters, and show considerable potential. Kadri has only played in 4 games, having just been promoted from the Marlies. Brent is a hard worker, and has contributed as a penalty killer. I am disappointed that the others, Hanson, Mitchell, and Zigomanis have thus far struggled for ice time.

A solution to the problems generated by the weakness of the centre position is essential for a successful season.

Left Wing

During the first quarter of the season, there have been four players skating on the left wing for the Leafs. Here are their stats.

	Goals	Assists	Points
Caputi	0	0	0
Kulemin	7	6	13
Sjostrom	1	1	2
MacArthur	7	11	18
Totals	**15**	**18**	**33**

Clarke MacArthur is the Leafs' leading scorer at the quarter pole. He has been a very pleasant addition to the team, having been acquired in the off-season from the Atlanta Thrashers. Nik Kulemin is beginning to show some signs of emerging as a forceful player on the team. Sjostrom has done some very good work as a checking forward. Caputi has not met with much success, and has just been sent back down to the Marlies for more seasoning on the farm club.

Right Wing

Five players are listed on the Leaf roster at the Right Wing position. Here is a summary of their production to date.

	Goals	Assists	Points
Brown	1	2	3
Kessel	9	4	13
Orr	2	0	2
Versteeg	6	6	12
Armstrong	1	0	1
Totals	**19**	**12**	**31**

It is well known fact that Phil Kessel is the so-called "franchise player" for the Leafs. Brian Burke gave up TWO first round draft picks to acquire him from the Boston Bruins. The search is still on to find someone, somewhere who can play on his line and consistently get the puck to this talented player who is known for his scoring prowess. Until this void is filled, Kessel will, I'm afraid, fall short of all our expectations. He had a very frustrating seven-game scoring drought in the first quarter-season

Kris Versteeg, is another new player who joined the Leafs in the summer from the Stanley Cup Champion Chicago Blackhawks. After a very tentative start to the season, he has recently begun to make a much stronger showing as a scorer. I anticipate further progress as the schedule unfolds.

Brown and Orr are the team's designated "tough guys". Orr is the enforcer, a role usually carried by one player on each team. Colby Armstrong, who came to Toronto from the Carolina Hurricanes, has been injured, and has only appeared in 8 games. Once he returns to action, he is capable of adding some more punch to the Leafs' attack.

<u>Summary</u>

Having played 20 games in an 82-game season, the Leafs have earned 19 points of a possible 40. Their winning percentage is 47.5.

Last year at this same juncture, they had 12 points, and a 30% rate of success.

It is clear that the current season presents us with much more reason for optimism than we had last November.

This morning's <u>Toronto Star</u> paints a very bleak picture of this year's team. The writer of the feature article has pretty well written off any hope of post-season play.

<u>I respectfully disagree with such a position!</u> I am confident that this current Leaf team can have a better second quarter than the first. If that happens, my optimism will continue.

I am hopeful that when Dion Phaneuf and Colby Armstrong are able to return to action, the team stability will grow, and good things will evolve with the passage of time. Furthermore, I am confident that Brian Burke and his staff will do their utmost to build upon what has materialized thus far, and make further alterations to the roster that will achieve their objective of making the playoffs next Spring.

<u>I refuse to give up</u> on this year's Maple Leafs at this early point in the season.

I am <u>NOT</u> a quitter!

Starting Off on the Wrong Foot

Utter disappointment! That is the only way to describe how I feel in the wake of last evening's loss to the Buffalo Sabres.

What the Sam Hill is it about Buffalo? Every stinking time that the Leafs cross the border to meet the Sabres, they get their collective butts kicked! It happens so frequently that it is beyond being a bad joke. It's almost to the point where the Leafs should just mail the two points over to Buffalo, and never mind playing the game.

Last night was no different. In the first period, the Leafs put themselves behind the eight ball early, when Colton Orr took a triple minor for roughing, followed closely by Kris Versteeg being banished for elbowing. Bang! Bang! Two power play goals within two minutes from the sticks of Leopold and Vanek. That was all that was needed. Another goal scored in the third period by Kaleta was just icing on the cake.

Although the Leafs picked up the pace during the second and third periods, one never got the impression that they were dangerous in any way. And, of course, one must not lose sight of the fact that they were facing Ryan Miller in the Buffalo net. He is one of the best goalies in the league, and he has had the Leafs' number for a long time now.

Phil Kessel's unassisted tenth goal of the season meant nothing in this game, other than denying Miller a shutout.

If you'll excuse my French, this was a helluva way to start the second quarter. We all know how desperately the Leafs need points. They MUST close the gap between themselves and the teams that hold a qualifying position for the playoffs. A winning streak of four or five games would put them right back into the thick of things, but letting points slip away will doom them. If the Leafs aren't within a point or two of a playoff spot by the end of December, they are SUNK! **AGAIN!**

The Leafs are now in Ottawa as this is written. They take on the Senators tonight. This game is another of the "must-win" variety. It will not be an easy game. The Sens got beaten up last night, too, so they will be out to avenge that defeat in front of their home fans. I am looking forward to the game. I hope that it will resemble last Saturday's match against Montreal, in terms of its pace at least.

And…I hope that the Leafs come out of it on top!

Leafs Suffer Fifth Shutout - The Slide Continues

I went to bed early last night. Oh yes, I DID watch the entire Leafs - Senators hockey game, The result, indicated above, was the main reason that I decided the best thing to do was go to bed, and get to sleep as quickly as possible.

I rather doubt that Brian Burke was able to follow the same course of action. He is probably losing a lot of sleep these nights, considering how his hockey players are letting him down. They are letting EVERYBODY down these nights...their fans, their management staff, their coaches...but most importantly THEMSELVES!

Before I began writing today's entry in my journal, I pondered the questions that MUST be going through Brian Burke's mind... **"What kind of situation do I have on my hands here? What is really going on? What must I do to get things turned around?"**

I will venture answers to the first two of those questions.

We have a very serious situation here. The ship is foundering on the rocks. With every loss, the Leafs' chances of recovery diminish accordingly. Burke has really tried hard to assemble a competitive team. Sadly though, these relatively talented players have, at least over the past few games, lost sight of the concept of playing as a team. THEY ARE NOT HELPING ONE ANOTHER. THEY ARE TRYING TO SOLVE THE PROBLEM BY THEMSELVES, AND <u>**THAT APPROACH IS DOOMED TO FAILURE FROM THE START.**</u>

To support this point of view, I undertook a bit of research. I took a good look at the league's three top scorers, Sidney Crosby, Steven Stamkos, and Alex Ovechkin. Specifically, I wanted to find out how much help these guys are getting as they rack up their tallies. I totaled up the ASSISTS garnered by every team-mate of each who had ten or more "helpers". Here is what I found:

Crosby, and three of his team-mates have a total of 65 assists.
Stamkos, and four of his, have 73 assists.
Ovechkin, and three other Capitals, have a total of 61 assists.

Clarke MacArthur is the top scorer for the Leafs. He and Grabovski have a total of 22 assists.   DO YOU GET MY POINT? DO THOSE STATS NOT INDICATE A LACK OF TEAMWORK WITHIN THE MAPLE LEAF CLUB?

I don't have an answer to the third question that I asked above. I don't know what Burke can do to turn things around.

A few games ago, Burke recalled Nazem Kadri from the minors to try and kick-start the team. At first, things looked promising, Kadri scored four assists in his first three games. Over the last two games, though, production has dried up again. It would be grossly unfair to presume that the kid from London can carry this team on his back.

While we're talking about the Marlies, it is noteworthy to point out that the Leaf farm club is doing reasonably well these days. After 23 games, they have earned 27 points…eight more than the parent club, and have scored 68 goals…twenty-one more than the Leafs.

Is there any possibility that Burke can pry Brad Richards away from the Dallas Stars? There has been talk in the media that such a move MIGHT be possible at some time down the line. Can it be accelerated?

Should a coaching change be contemplated? Have the Leafs stopped listening to Ron Wilson? How effective are some of the Assistant Coaches?

If Wilson is the problem here, then he must go, Whether he is fired outright, or bumped upstairs, his interactions with the players must be tempered if they have become too abrasive. Such a move would be agonizing for Burke, since he and Wilson are such good personal friends. If Wilson id NOT the problem, then his assistants should have THEIR roles in the situation assessed. Any negative influences must be eliminated, and if firings or reassignments are called for, then so be it.

There is no doubt in my mind that the serious injuries suffered by Colby Armstrong and Dion Phaneuf have been very detrimental to the team's fortunes. Their return to the lineup will be welcome. However, I am worried that the team's troubles run deeper than the return of these two players is able to cure. I am becoming more and more convinced that significant decisions by the management team are going to be needed in order to get things where they need to be.

Tomorrow night, the Tampa Bay Lightning will visit the Air Canada Centre. Their five top guns (Stamkos, St. Louis, Purcell, Malone, and Downie) have accumulated 115 scoring points in their first quarter season. I am having trouble trying to be optimistic about the outcome of the game.

A few of my friends and acquaintances have thrown in the towel on this year's edition of the Leafs. Even though I have pointed out to them that they are currently in a much better position than they were at this time last year, they are not convinced that the club has a very good chance to get into the playoffs. I certainly understand their sense of futility, but, to this point in time at least, I do not share it.

I desperately want this team to succeed!

Stunning Loss Difficult to Take

Question: What was that loud, sucking sound that I heard just before ten o'clock last night?

Possible Answers:
(a)   The sound of a single point being flushed into the sewer system beneath the ACC.
(b)   The gasp of disbelief as the hometown crowd witnessed another defeat being snatched from the jaws of victory.
(c)   Another glimmer of hope for a successful season rushing through the exits in advance of a disappointed and disheartened audience.
(d)   All of the above.

As the time clock ticked down late in the third period of last night's game, I had a sickening premonition of what was about to happen. And then it happened! In an absolutely incredible and horrifying space of eighty-five seconds on the clock, the Leafs surrendered two goals, and an almost certain win became an overtime loss. The television cameras caught several images that pretty well summed up the emotions of the moment:
   *   Jonas Gustavsson smashing his goalie stick over the crossbar of his net,
   *   Ron Wilson beating his customary rapid retreat from behind the bench,
   *   Brian Burke's head disappearing from view as he once again undoubtedly uttered an expletive or two about the raw anguish he felt about the game's outcome, and
   *   A second outburst of anger and frustration as Gustavsson pounded the wall with his new goalie stick on his way to the dressing room.

The Maple Leafs had outplayed and outscored the Tampa Bay Lightning in this game. They were within nine seconds of a win, thanks to two goals from Kulemin and another by Versteeg. Gustavsson, Schenn, and Kulemin, along with several other Leafs, had played a reasonably good game, and they definitely deserved to win. And suddenly, everything went wrong!

Two quick goals by Martin St. Louis in regulation time, and Simon Gagne in overtime, spelled an end to a potential happy celebration of another home victory. It was a perfect testimony to the ugly way the hockey gods dole out their wickedness. Burke must wonder what he has to do to get things turned around. Wilson must be beside himself with frustration. The club has no time to wallow in despair. The Edmonton Oilers will be coming to town on Thursday for one of their rare visits to the ACC. The Leafs absolutely MUST gain these next two points, or else we'll be in the same boat we were in last year, watching the season slip away, point after point after point.

December 3, 2010   **Game #24   Oilers 5   Leafs 0**

Rock Bottom!

Wasn't that one gawd-awful display of hockey at the ACC last night? It was absolutely pathetic! I could scarcely believe what I was seeing.

The Edmonton Oilers had come to town. They were brimming with excitement. They arrived within hours after laying a beating on the Montreal Canadiens, and were equally looking forward to playing against another iconic (ha, ha) franchise in front of a packed crowd. Young (19) rookie Taylor Hall had purchased 30 tickets for friends and family to see the game.

Sitting at home, watching on Leafs TV, I sensed trouble early in the game, when Jordan Eberle scored on a soft backhand that Gustavsson should have easily stopped. In the second period, he let in another stinker off the stick of Hall, and was lifted after facing a mere six shots. When Giguere was beaten by Sam Gagner for the third Edmonton goal later in the middle frame, the game was essentially over. The Oilers administered the "coup de grace" with two quick goals by Hall and Jones late in the third.

In the final stages of the game, the hometown crowd was booing the Leafs unmercifully. They were screaming "Fire Wilson!" at the top of their lungs. The Leafs themselves were distraught with their own ineptitude. They had played a horrible game, and they all knew it…to the very last man.

This was an unmitigated disaster. The Oilers came into this game tied with the Leafs in 28th place in the NHL. They had the worst defensive record in the league, with 92 goals against. This should have been an easy two points for the Leafs, but they played like a bunch of midgets.

These guys would never admit to the media that they have quit on their coaching staff… but their actions speak louder than words. I watched the first period, almost aghast at the disorganized way that they were playing. When that first softie went in past "The Monster", I feared the worst. There was NOTHING in the way of a threat emanating from the Leafs. They stunk! There is no other way to sum it up!

Tomorrow night, the Leafs play host to the Bruins…the team with the BEST defensive record in the NHL. I can feel the dread building within me with each passing hour as the match draws near. As if this prospect isn't bad enough, next week Toronto faces the Penguins and the Capitals in their own buildings. Sidney Crosby is presently single-handedly tearing the league apart with his scoring prowess. After facing off against Sidney and his buddies, they have to confront Alexander Ovechkin and his band of merry men.

Oh death…where is thy sting???

Kessel Salts Leaf Win in Shootout

What a difference a couple of days can make in hockey! On Thursday evening, the Maple Leafs played a disgraceful game and were severely taken to task by a sellout crowd at the Air Canada Centre. They had been shellacked by the Edmonton Oilers. They were booed off the ice by their irate fans. The crowd screamed for the head of Ron Wilson on a platter. It was a catastrophic loss, to say the very least.

Last night, the Leafs came out of the gate with a determination that they have dearly lacked in several of their recent games. When Nathan Horton scored the first Boston goal, it looked like the Leafs were beginning to dig a hole for themselves, as has been the case on so many previous occasions. However, tonight was going to be different. With just four minutes left in the first period, Carl Gunnarsson teamed up with Tyler Bozak and Nazem Kadri to tie the score.

There were no goals scored by either club in the second period. Early in the third, Gregory Campbell put the visitors ahead. Things began to look a little grim for the home team, thanks to an absolutely brilliant performance in goal by Tim Thomas, the 36 year-old goalie in the Boston net. He is having a career year so far this season. His team boasts the best defensive record in the NHL, and Thomas has been absolutely marvelous in the Beantown net.

Tonight, however, the Leafs were not going to be denied. With less than a minute left in the game, Kris Versteeg capped a furious assault on the Boston net by slamming a rebound past Thomas, sending the game to overtime. The five-minute, four-on-four extra session solved nothing, so the decision rested on the outcome of a shootout.

Phil Kessel turned out to be the player who prevailed in the shootout session. He fired a shot at Thomas that was so hard it propelled the goalie backwards into the net, carrying the puck in with him under his pads. Game over!

The Leafs played hard all night. They were rewarded by a standing ovation, and they raised their sticks skywards in appreciation. They had rebounded in fine fashion from the horror of their most recent outing. But…can they keep the momentum going? I have great concerns about that.

Their next two games pits the team against the Washington Capitals and the Pittsburgh Penguins in two consecutive road matches. They will be the clear underdogs in both of those contests. This team remains very fragile. They are not showing very much potential of a strong offence. The road ahead is long and steep, and, if they are going to have success, several players MUST develop more offensive output…and they'll have to do it SOON! They did well last night, but they have to keep things rolling, and that is going to be tough for them to accomplish.

Leafs Stun Caps With Late Surge

Let me begin today's journal entry by giving our beloved Maple Leafs full credit for their remarkable late-game heroics that resulted in a much needed win in Washington D.C. last night. The team should be lauded for their never-give-up attitude, and their sixty-plus minutes of effort that, for once, was rewarded with a victory over a team currently sitting in SECOND PLACE in the NHL standings.

However, dear readers, I want to issue a word or two of caution. Let's not get sucked into such a state of euphoria that we allow ourselves to be injured by jumping on and off the Leaf bandwagon. Yes, the Leafs have just thrilled us with two straight shootout wins. But…have you looked at the schedule in the past couple of days? If you have, you will notice that before ten o'clock this Saturday evening, they will have faced Pittsburgh, Philadelphia, and Montreal in very quick succession. I would strongly suggest that we all wait until those three games have been played before we get too excited.

Last night turned out to be quite exciting for all of us, but upon reflection, we shouldn't forget that the score was 4 to 1 for the Caps at the beginning of the third period. Mathieu Perrault had ripped two goals past Jonas Gustavsson and Alex (The Great 8) Ovechkin had blazed in another. Clarke MacArthur had the lone Leaf marker. There was very little indication of what was to come in the final stanza.

First, Mikhail Grabovski slapped in his sixth goal of the season, ably assisted by Kaberle and Kulemin. That got the Leafs back into the match. The game plodded along for another thirteen minutes or so with no further scoring. It appeared that the Caps would be able to close things out with minimal effort. WRONG!

With less than two and a half minutes left, Tim Brent put his third goal of the season past Neuwirth in the Caps net, and the home team was suddenly in trouble. Ron Wilson then pulled Gustavsson to the Leaf bench, and MacArthur slammed the tying goal past Neuwirth with only 24 seconds on the clock. Five minutes of overtime failed to produce a winner, and another shootout was upon us. Mikhail Grabovski, the second shooter for Toronto, scored the winning goal, while his Swedish buddy held the fort in the Leaf net, blanking all three Washington marksmen.

The team certainly deserves our applause for two great efforts since hitting rock bottom just last week. I am also delighted that the infamous gods of hockey have given them a break or two. Nonetheless, the road ahead leads uphill. The Leafs have allowed themselves to be outclassed by most of their opponents, and their standing remains low. When…and only when they start accumulating points in bunches can we allow ourselves to begin regaining the confidence and optimism that we mistakenly grasped early in the schedule. We need to hold the feet of these players to the fire until they prove to be the playoff team that Brian Burke told us that they were.

Pens Win Eleventh Straight Over Listless Leafs

I honestly don't think that very many people expected the Leafs to beat the Pittsburgh Penguins in their own rink last night. Sure enough...they didn't! Everyone who follows hockey knows very well that Sidney Crosby is on a scoring rampage that is almost awe-inspiring to witness. Even his team-mates are being quoted on television that they are captivated by the skill and creativity that the young man brings to the game night in and night out. He is clearly the most remarkable superstar in the NHL at the present time, and is on his way to having an outstanding season...barring unforeseen injury.

Of course, with Sid the Kid performing at such a level, the rest of the Penguins are performing very well, too. They don't want to be perceived as a bunch of players riding on the coattails of their young (23) captain. And we must not forget that two of their best colleagues, Malkin and Staal, are still recovering from injuries. When those two return, the Pens have the potential to go a long way in the playoffs, for sure.

The Leafs were not very good last night at all. Things picked up for them in the third period, with Grabovski and Bozak scoring to make the result look respectable, but in reality, they played poorly. Crosby had two goals, Letestu had two more, and Pascal Dupuis netted one. Once the home team had built up a 4 - 0 lead, there was very little hope of any Leaf comeback...especially considering the inept play of the Maple Leafs.

Now readers, I want to tell you that I don't make a habit of listening to very many call-in shows that can be found on the radio these days. However, yesterday I just happened to be in the car a lot, what with travelling around doing Christmas shopping, etc. Naturally, I punched up the Fan 590 as we travelled here and there on our seasonal mission. It is clear that there are a lot of very unhappy Toronto Maple Leaf followers out there, based upon what I heard on the air as we drove along.

I, too, am unhappy. Earlier this year, I asked for, and received official permission to attend as many as one Leaf practice per month, starting in October. A personal matter kept me from attending any practices in October, and part of November. Recently though, I have not ventured to the Mastercard Centre because it is becoming more and more evident that the team is in near-crisis mode, and I don't wish to intrude on such an unhappy situation. While I have not yet written off this year's team, with each accumulating loss the handwriting on the wall gets clearer. Sooner or later, I rather expect that more changes are coming down the pipe.

What are the changes going to be? I have no idea. I would only be guessing. But, they will come, I'm sure. The present situation in untenable. With Christmas upon us, we will have to wait a little longer, but change within this non-cohesive hockey club are just around the corner. **Right, Mr. Burke???**

Hope is Fading Fast

Leaf Captain Dion Phaneuf returned to action last night against the Philadelphia Flyers after missing 16 games because of the very serious cut to his leg. He assisted on the only Leaf goal, scored by Mikhail Grabovski in the second period.

Other than that, nothing much happened.

I DID watch the game on television last night. As time went along, a singular thought kept coursing through my mind. **"Nothing is happening out there on that ice!"**

The Leafs were not scoring. The Leafs were shooting…but were missing the net…almost entirely! The pace of the game was brisk on the part of both teams, but the Leafs efforts were unproductive. They were skating miles, and accomplishing nothing.

There was little, if any, evidence that the Leafs had been coached and prepared for the Flyers. They were outplayed and outclassed by the visiting team. Daniel Briere, once thought to be too small to ever become an effective NHL player, scored twice. The other Philly goals were notched by Leno and Pronger.

After the game, I saw one interview with Brett Lebda aired on Leafs TV. He identified all of the areas of the game that the Leafs SHOULD HAVE performed, but ruefully had to admit that they had not been up to the task.

That, I'm afraid, is what we are going to be in for as the rest of the 2010 -2011 schedule is played out. With 54 games remaining, the Leafs presently consist of a bunch of players who can talk the talk…but can't walk the walk! Since the beginning of the season, goals-per-game have diminished from a high of 2.5 to their present low of 1.6. Their opponents have outscored them by a margin of 23 goals. Their success rate has plunged from 100 percent to their current standing of 43 percent.

The Leaf forwards have not been able to score adequately. The team has been let down badly by a high-priced, but largely inept defence. In recent games, both goalies who have performed with reasonable competence and effectiveness have begun to show their frustration. I am now prepared to state outright that the coaching staff no longer has the ears of the team. Their ineffectiveness is manifest almost every time out. Even in terms of three-star selections, Leafs have been chosen FIVE TIMES of a possible TWENTY-FOUR.

If the Leafs were to win every game played before the end of December, their winning percentage would be only 55. **Readers, I regret to say that hope for a successful season is almost gone!**

Leafs Outwork Tired Hab Crew for a Win

In his post-game remarks last night, Ron Wilson informed the media that he was going to do his Christmas shopping today. The only thing that he was unsure about was whether he would be shopping in the mode of a Santa Clause or a Scrooge. Well, thanks to an energetic outing at the ACC that resulted in a well-earned victory, Wilson will be in at least a semi-jolly frame of mind. The visitors were dead tired, having played, and lost, the night before. Coach Jacques Martin decided to give star goalie Carey Price the night off, and Alex Auld replaced him in goal. The Leafs got out of the gate quickly, and scored the first two goals of the game, giving themselves a real lift, for once.

The two first-period scorers were Phil Kessel and Thomas Kaberle. Kessel was positioned right beside the net to drive a rebound past Auld for the first marker. Then, just a couple of minutes later, Kaberle took a perfect pass on the fly, and drove another past the Hab netminder.

There was no more scoring until late in the second period, when Mike Cammalleri potted his tenth of the season to get the Canadiens back into the game. The final goal of the contest was scored into an empty net by Kris Versteeg, and that one sealed the deal for the home club.

The Leafs have a day off today before they fly to Edmonton, where they will open a three-day swing against the Oilers, the Flames, and the Canucks. They absolutely have to pick up the majority of the points available from those three games. They have reached the point in their schedule when every point has maximum importance. Even as it is, the Christmas season is not going to be as jolly as any of us had hoped.

If the Leafs do not earn 4 of the 6 points available on their road trip to the west, their journey will be, for all intents and purposes, a waste of time. Both Edmonton and Calgary are tied for last position in the Western Conference, each with 27 points. The Leafs currently have 26 points. One thing is certain. With these three bad teams facing off against one another, we'll soon know which one is the worst of the bunch. Isn't THAT a great way to skate into the coming festive season?

Visions of sugar plums? I don't think so! Not this Christmas, anyway. Along with almost everyone in the Leaf Nation, I am very disappointed with the lack of positive development that this Maple Leaf team has demonstrated thus far this season. The serious injuries sustained by Dion Phaneuf and Colby Armstrong have significantly factored into the team's problems, but things have been exacerbated by disappointing performances by a number of individual players. Also, in recent games, I have become more and more convinced that the entire coaching staff has become irrelevant. Unless the Leafs can turn things around in dramatic fashion in the immediate future, I expect that coaching changes might be in the offing at some early point in the new year.

Leafs Get Revenge Against Scrappy Oiler Crew

The last time that these two youthful hockey teams met, it was at the ACC, on one of the rare visits that the Oilers make to Toronto. The Leafs had an off-night, and the Oilers clobbered them 5 to zip. That was the game that I have delineated in red ink on my progress chart as the one in which the Leafs hit rock bottom.

Last night, I am happy to say, the Maple Leafs exacted a bit of revenge. They mounted what I felt was a genuine team effort, and put the boots to the home team, right in their own rink. J. S. Giguere was as solid as a rock in the Leaf net. At the other end, Khabibulin (the Bulin Wall) was also very good. He really had little or no chance of stopping at least three of the Toronto goals (Phaneuf, Grabovski, & Kessel). Giguere made several exceptionally good saves.

The Leafs were also well served by their blue line contingent. Phaneuf set the tone for his team by blasting a point shot past Khabibulin. He, aided by staunch performances from Beauchemin, Kaberle, and Schenn, kept the Oilers at bay.

Ten different Leafs earned points in last night's match, with Kessel and Versteeg both having two-point nights. That is a feature of games that I like to see. When a whole bunch of players can produce points, the opposition can't afford to focus upon any one individual in terms of defence. When a significant number of different players on a team can score, it serves as a tremendous morale booster for the club as a whole.

Toronto now journeys into the mild climes of Southern Alberta to face the Flames on Thursday evening. The Flames are in as much trouble as are their visitors when it comes to earning a spot in the post-season. They have struggled since the first of the season. Some of their players have not performed up to expectation. They traded Ian White away to Carolina. Matt Stajan was a healthy scratch for their last game. The fans are howling for the heads of both Sutter brothers who are managing and coaching the team.

With two games remaining on this western road trip, the Maple Leafs absolutely MUST win one of them. If they lose both, their progress in the standings will stall once again. That is something that they just can't afford to let happen. They remain a fragile club, with several players still needing to play their best style of game. If the boys can approach the Calgary contest with the same attitude that they showed last night, they can lock up the points that they have to get, and then focus on beating the Sedin boys and their pals on "Hockey Night in Canada" this coming Saturday.

Flames Blast Leafs with Three Goals in a Minute

I didn't watch last night's tilt between the Leafs and the Flames. From what I saw on TV and read about the game on the internet this morning, I didn't miss much. The Flames showed up for the game, and the Leafs played another softie.

Head coach Ron Wilson, in his post-game remarks, admitted that the Leafs weren't very good for the first two periods.. I suggest that, when a team allows three goals in a time span of 57 seconds, that is an understatement. The game was tied 1 - 1 until just after the fifteen minute mark of the second period. If the Leafs had been able to take that tie with them into the third period, we can only speculate on what might have happened

But no…! Bang! Bang! Bang! Suddenly the score became 4 - 1 for the home team. The game was essentially over. Even though they exchanged single markers in the third, the Leafs didn't have enough jam to get themselves back into the game. Wilson remarked that only one of the Leafs' forward lines had anything going, and that was Grabovski's line. The others didn't contribute anything. This was yet another night of wheel spinning.

I cannot, for the life of me, understand how the Leafs can let some of the slowest ranked teams in the NHL off the hook when they come up against them. They come in to some of these games with a ripe opportunity to make up points, and they just seem to squirrel them away. They claim to have pride in their team, and confidence in their abilities, but time and time again, they fail to perform in key situations. It absolutely boggles my mind!

If this road trip is going to amount to anything at all, the Leafs must go into Vancouver for the game tomorrow night, and beat the Canucks on their own pond. That is a tall order. The Canucks have been doing very well lately, and they are usually very good in front of their home crowd. However, the Leafs SHOULD be motivated to give them a fight.

The Leafs have only two games left to play before Christmas. Unless they can step up and compete, there will be a lot of stockings filled with coal next Saturday morning.

Stinkers like last night's effort should never happen considering everything that's at stake for the blue and white!

Canucks Overpower a Spunky Leaf Effort

I'd like to start off my journal entry this morning by giving the Leafs a pat on the back for the sincere effort that they put into the game against Vancouver last night. They DID try their best, but really, it was almost too much to expect them to beat the Canucks in front of their home crowd. They should have taken advantage of a less competent club when they paired off against Calgary the other night. However, that's not the way things worked out, and their road trip to the Great Canadian West has turned out to be a bit of a bust. Oh, well…!

I decided to do a bit of research this morning to try and understand exactly what the Leafs were up against last night. I sat down at my computer, and did a side-by -side, man-by-man comparison of the two teams. Here are the numbers

The Canucks have played 26 skaters thus far this season.
The Leafs have played 27.

Vancouver has scored 96 goals…26 more than Toronto.

The Westerners are credited with 165 assists…the Eastern team a mere 120.

The Canucks overpower the Leafs by a total point differential of 71. This bit of investigating serves to give us all a clearer understanding of the realities that underlie last night's result.

The only Leaf who scored last night was Grabovski, assisted by Kulemin and MacArthur. Vancouver got markers from Burrows, Hansen, Ehrhoff, and Henrik Sedin. It was an entertaining game, but the Leafs really did deserve a better fate than they got. The Eastern visitors never let up as far as their effort was concerned.

Only one game remains before Christmas. That one will be played at the ACC next Tuesday night against the Atlanta Thrashers. Win or lose, the Maple Leafs, management, coaches, and players alike will not have the merriest of Christmases. This team remains under a very dark cloud. A winning percentage of 43 is simply not good enough to realistically contend for the post-season.

The Maple Leafs need a WINNING STREAK in the worst of ways. They started out the season with a four-game winning streak. Since that one was broken at Game #5, they have been unable to win more than two in a row. That won't cut it! They need six or seven in a row…just to build up their confidence and morale.

There is still time…but they can't afford to fumble around for too much longer. They are rapidly closing in on CALAMITY!

Leafs Fall Farther in Eastern Conference Standings

I am now CERTAIN that the Leafs are not going to have a very Merry Christmas.

I'm not just talking about the players. I'm talking about everyone…players…coaches… management…EVERYONE! This team is in bad shape…REALLY BAD SHAPE! Last year, at the Christmas Break, their winning percentage was 44.7. **This year, it's 42.4!**   **See what I mean?**

Last night, they lost their third game in a row. The Thrashers pounded them 6 to 3. As we have seen before, the Leafs got off to an absolutely lousy start, standing around in their own end, watching the Thrashers buzz around them like a swarm of bees, popping two of their first three shots behind Gustavsson, who was clearly not comfortable in the net from the get-go.

The Leafs were always behind in this one. At the end of the first, the score was 2 - 0, thanks to Atlanta goals by Modin and Enstrom. John Mitchell got his first goal of the season in the second, but that was offset by Another Modin goal, his second of the night. The Thrashers put the game away with two third period markers from he sticks of Stewart and Enstrom. The Leafs put on a bit of a rally with goals from Grabovski and Kulemin, but an empty-netter by Ladd stifled the home club once and for all.

I would be remiss if I didn't say a word of congratulations to Tomas Kaberle, whose second assist of the night on Grabovski's goal was the 500th point in his career. THAT IS A REMARKABLE ACHIEVEMENT. Well done, Tomas!

Getting back to the situation at hand, I simply cannot imagine that Brian Burke and his management team will sit still, and do nothing to try and turn things around before it is too late. Burke said, just yesterday, that there appears to be little or nothing on the horizon as far as trades are concerned. There are no suitable players available who would make a difference. That being the case, I have a suggestion.

CHANGE THE COACHING STAFF1   Re-assign Ron Wilson to another role within the organization, or buy out his contract. I believe that there is an insurmountable generation gap between the coaches and the players.

Hire either Dallas Eakins or Doug Gilmour as the new head coach. Allow the new coach to retain any assistant that he believes to be competent, and hire anyone he wishes to help him build the Maple Leafs into a competitive hockey team.

In making this recommendation, I do so without any malice towards the incumbent coaching staff. It's strictly business. This coaching staff has had plenty of opportunity to accomplish Burke's objective, and that hasn't happened. The time for change has come.

Leafs Snow Devils in New Jersey Blizzard

Yesterday was not a good day for a lot of people in the New Jersey area. Outside, the weather was crumby. A howling blizzard was buffeting the entire Eastern Seaboard. Transportation was in a state of near paralysis, with air transportation grounded, rail traffic slowed markedly, and land transportation next to impossible. Inside the Prudential Centre in Newark, New Jersey, the crowd assembled to witness the NHL game between the Devils and the Maple Leafs was estimated to number somewhere between 2500 and 5000. Most of those brave souls who had struggled through the storm to get to the game were destined to be disappointed...again.

Neither the Devils nor the Leafs are having very good seasons...at least not at this juncture in the long NHL schedule. New Jersey had won only nine games since the season began. They had lost twenty-four. Just last week, Manager Lou Lamiorello had fired his rookie coach, John MacLean, and summoned Jacques Lemaire to replace him on an interim basis, at least. To put it bluntly, the Devils are having a devil of a season.

The Leafs, as we are all too aware, are not doing a heck of a lot better. While the Devils are at rock bottom of the Eastern Conference standings, the Leafs are only marginally above them. The hometown fans in T.O. are howling for the coach's head too. The Leafs absolutely MUST start winning in bunches if they are going to even hope to get into the playoffs next spring. Many fans have already written the team off.

On this occasion, the Leafs turned out to be the better of the two weak teams. Thanks to a two-goal performance by Colby Armstrong, and singles contributed by John Mitchell and Nik Kulemin, the visitors prevailed. Kris Versteeg also had a two-point night, chipping in with a pair of assists. The only response offered by a very discouraged home team came off the stick of Rod Pelley.

In goal, it was a good night for Jonas Gustavsson, and a lousy one for Martin Brodeur. The latter, who is arguably one of the greatest goalies in NHL history, has had a very unfortunate campaign to this point in the schedule. He has been bothered by some minor injury problems, and has not been particularly sharp on rare occasions. There has even been the suggestion that he might welcome a trade to another team in the near future. Time will tell.

The Leafs have two more games this week to end the Calendar year. Both are home matches, They will entertain Carolina tomorrow evening, followed by Columbus on Thursday. Both of those games have to be regarded as must-wins. The boys in blue and white have dug themselves a deep hole, and they will have to really start putting together some team efforts if they want to climb in the standings.

A Moral Victory…But a Real Life Loss

By now, we have all become familiar with the Maple Leafs' proclivity for tire –spinning. For several hours over the past couple of days, they participated in a lot of such activity. After playing the New Jersey Devils the other night in the middle of an East Coast blizzard, they spent five hours marooned on a bus, several more stranded in their hotel, and then even more on a frustrating trip home from Newark to Toronto.

Arriving back in Ontario just in time to play against the Carolina Hurricane, the boys donned their home blue uniforms, and skated onto the ACC ice as prepared as they could make themselves to take on their well-rested opponents.

Under the circumstances…very unfavourable circumstances indeed, the Leafs played fairly well against the Hurricane. Sadly, though, they were not able to come out of this game on top. For a while, with the score tied 3 – 3, I was hoping that they could hold on and claim at least the single point that a tie would have brought them. However, a late goal by Patrick Dwyer put the visitors ahead, and the exhausted home team was unable to put any more pucks past Cam Ward in the Hurricane net.

The Leafs got goals from two of their most reliable marksmen. Phil Kessel scored two goals in the first period, and Mikhail Grabovski notched the only goal of the second period. The first three Carolina goals were scored by Eric Staal (2) and Jeff Skinner. Even though the home team lost, this was an entertaining game, and it isn't easy to say negative things about any team that plays so well just after experiencing such a horrendous day and a half in the grips of one of the worst storms on record for the Eastern seaboard.

Six more games must be played before the Leafs reach the half-way point in their schedule. They absolutely have to put a streak together in a hurry. Every point that they fail to achieve from this point on is equivalent to a nail in their coffin. I am trying my very best to keep my hopes up for a resurgence of what we saw in the first four games of the season, but time is NOT on the side of these hopes any more. The Leafs deserve a winning streak based upon their attitude alone, but it has to be earned by hitting the twine to stop the clock. All else falls short of the mark.

Next up for the Leafs will be the Columbus Blue Jackets. This will be another home game tomorrow evening. Like the home team, Columbus does not occupy a playoff berth as yet, but the Blue Jackets HAVE won five more games than Toronto. This game will not be any sort of pushover. The Maple Leafs earned a lot of credit for their valiant effort last night, but tomorrow will be a whole new story. They had better knuckle down and earn a "W" against their Western Conference foes tomorrow, or else the tire-spinning will just go on…and on…and on!

Leafs Run Out of Gas Against the Blue Jackets

Last night was a rare occasion in our house. Our daughter, Colleen was home for a brief holiday visit, and she. her mother, and I were all gathered in the living room chatting. The television was, naturally, tuned in to the Maple Leaf-Columbus hockey game.

Suddenly, Colleen pointed toward the television screen and asked, "What do the letters CBJ stand for?"

"The Columbus Blue Jackets," I responded.

"Where is Columbus? Do they have an NHL team?"

That brief exchange was a terse reminder of situations that have occurred before in Maple Leaf history. Last night was not the first time that the Leafs have entertained rare appearances by a small-market, Western Conference team, and allowed them to take control of the game.

Clubs like the Blue Jackets just LOVE to play at the Air Canada Centre. They regard that rink to be almost like a cathedral. Every NHL player knows that Toronto is one of the main stops in the NHL, and they ALL want to put on a good show because of the usual wide media coverage that the games get there. Like many good hosts, the Leafs usually allow their guests the leverage that they need to make a positive impression.

Such was the case last night. The home team took advantage of their visitors in the early stages of the game, surging in front 2 to 1 with goals from Kulemin and Bozak. Then, they gradually let the game slip away. Two goals by Kristen Huselius, and another by R. J. Umberger gave the visitors a one-goal advantage, and Toronto was unable to tie the score. Another valuable two points slipped down the drain.

This was the EIGHTH time this season that the Leafs have lost by a single goal. If they had merely tied those eight games, they would have 38 points, and would be in 9th place in the Eastern Conference...within easy reach of a post-game position, given more than half of the season has yet to be played. If the Leafs had WON those eight games, their point total would be 46...placing them THIRD in the Conference.

However, those things didn't happen, and the Maple Leafs sit woefully near the bottom of league standings. As I retired for the evening after watching part of the post-game show, I felt genuinely sad about how the Leafs had surrendered these points to their opponents.

How valiantly will they perform when they journey to Ottawa for yet another skirmish in the "Battle of Ontario" on Saturday? We'll soon see!

Leafs Celebrate the New Year with a Win

Customarily, the arrival of the New Year is a time when many people decide to turn over a new leaf in their lives, either professionally or personally. They sit down and make resolutions that they aspire to fulfill. Sometimes, they choose not to divulge these goals to anyone, for fear of being held accountable by people other than themselves.

The Toronto Maple Leafs do not have that luxury of confidentiality. They must resolve to play better…significantly better in this new year of 2011. They must prove to their legion of fans that they really are a team on the march towards a better future. Right now, there are many who doubt that. They have not seen very much evidence that such is the case. Critics can look at the team's current statistics and conclude that this year's team is not even as good as last year's. Once again, playoff aspirations are very much in doubt.

Last night, on "Hockey Night in Canada" we saw two struggling teams go head to head in another episode of the Battle of Ontario. This time, the Leafs emerged victorious. The win was convincing, as the score above indicates, but it remains to be seen if the Leafs can use this timely victory as a turning point of any consequence. In order to do so, they must set upon a course of several wins in a row. They have, in the immortal words of poet Robert Frost, "miles to go before they sleep".

Like the Leafs, the Ottawa Senators are going through a very rough time. They stand marginally higher than Toronto in the Eastern Conference standings, but their play is away below the expectations of their fans. To make things even worse, they will be without Jason Spezza, one of their key players for the next few weeks due to a shoulder separation.

The Leafs dominated the Sens right from the start last evening. Clarke MacArthur opened the scoring early in the first period. Tyler Bozak, with assists from Phil Kessel and Joey Crabb, scored twice, extending the lead to 3 – 0 by the first intermission. In the second, Darryl Boyce got his first NHL goal, and Luke Schenn blasted a shot from the point to give the Leafs an insurmountable lead. Sergei Gonchar was the only Ottawa shooter to beat Jamie Reimer, who played a solid game in the Leaf net, with his proud mom and dad watching and snapping pictures from the stands.

This week, the Leafs play home games against Boston, on Monday, and St. Louis on Thursday. On Wednesday morning, my wife, Charlotte and I are looking forward to our very first visit to a Leaf practice at their new facility, the Mastercard Centre in Etobicoke. Following that occasion, I hope to be able to give my readers some additional insights behind the scenes with our favourite hockey club.

In the meantime, a win tomorrow against the big, bad Boston Bruins will add to the promise of a fresh start to the 2011 calendar year.

Another Unsuccessful Struggle

As the Maple Leaf schedule inches toward the halfway mark, I regret the need for me to record another one-goal loss for this year's team…the ninth such loss to date. The Boston Bruins enjoyed another night away from home last night, nipping the locals by a score of 2 to 1.

Mikhail Grabovski was the only Leaf able to register a goal against Tukka Rask, netminder for Boston for this occasion. His shot into the visitors' net resulted from a beautiful outlet pass from Luke Schenn. Unfortunately, this sole offering from the boys in blue and white came early in the game. While his mates tried desperately to add some insurance to the advantage they held at the first intermission, their efforts were met with futility. However, the Beantowners, specifically Nathan Horton and Marc Savard, were able to spoil a very well-played outing by young Jamie Reimer in the Leaf net.

At the beginning of the hockey season, GM Brian Burke promised the Leaf Nation a competitive team this year. He stated clearly that he, like all of us, was sick and tired of watching the crappy sort of play that we have grown accustomed to over the past few years. Well, folks, the Leafs aren't yet competitive. As of this writing, they stand 27th in a thirty-team league. Statistically, they are actually worse off than they were at this time last season. **How much longer do we have to wait???**

Tomorrow morning, I will be visiting the team at their practice facility in Etobicoke. While I have no way of knowing what this experience will be like, I honestly expect that, at some point, I may be asked to express a viewpoint or opinion or suggestion about what is needed to turn the team fortunes around. Here is one such matter that I believe should be addressed urgently.

The Leafs need a big. tough centreman to play on the same line as Phil Kessel.

Right now, Kessel is trying to do too much. He is lugging the puck up and down the ice, trying desperately to set up plays with his linemates, and at the same time attempting to position himself for shots on the net. Last night, he registered 8 shots on goal, yet scored not a single point. He needs a setup man…and he needed him YESTERDAY!

Who should Brian Burke move mountains to acquire? **BRAD RICHARDS**

As of today, Richards has scored 18 goals and 27 assists for the Dallas Stars. That's 45 points in 40 games…more than a point per game. Richards is a tough, gritty hockey player. He is a proven veteran player who, in my opinion, could help the Leafs from the moment of his arrival. Hang the expense! If the Stars are willing to part company with Richards, then I believe Burke should get him. **Brad Richards would be a decided asset for the Leafs NOW.**

A Cataclysmic Collapse in World Junior Hockey

Last evening, at approximately ten o'clock, as my wife and I were driving home from my dialysis treatment at Credit Valley Hospital, we crossed the railway tracks on the Ninth Line in Mississauga. As I glanced to the right, I saw the dazzling light of the locomotive on an approaching train. For an instant, a sudden pang of fear swept over me.

Less than an hour earlier, I had a similar sense of foreboding. I was watching the World Junior gold medal game being played at the HSBC Arena in Buffalo. The protagonists were Canada and Russia. It was midway through the second period. Canada appeared to be in control of the game. The score was 3 – 0, and yet another gold medal for the Canadians appeared to be in the bag.

Slowly, but surely I sensed a change in the flow of the game. It seemed that the pace of the action had slowed. Canadian pressure upon their opponents was diminishing. The boys in the brilliant red uniforms were no longer putting forth a real effort to extend their lead by adding any insurance markers.

Early in the third period, as television commentator Bob Mackenzie so aptly stated later, "All the wheels came off the bus at the same time". The Canadian pressure just stopped. Shooters stopped shooting. Checkers stopped checking. The Canadian boys were either running around chasing their shadows or standing around, watching their game slipping away. Avenues started opening, and the Russians started pouring through.

Suddenly, they scored. The Russians were back in the game. Then came another goal. It was a softy. Trouble…real trouble! The Canadian coach should have called a time-out to settle these kids down, and let them get their bearings. **He didn't!**

Then…bang! The score was tied! What in Sam Hill is going on here?????

At that point, my treatment was over, and I had to stop watching the game, and leave the care centre. By the time Charlotte and I got into our car, the Russians had taken the lead, and as we drove off hospital property out onto Eglinton Avenue, they nailed down their triumph by scoring their FIFTH goal in TEN shots. The Russian teenagers, some of them out of control with delirious joy, claimed their gold medals, and absolutely butchered their national anthem.

The Canadian Juniors had folded like a cheap tent! They will have to live with this ignominious defeat for a long time…probably the rest of their lives. A few of these players may get to experience other successes in their hockey lives. Some may someday win a Stanley Cup. Some may gain individual awards in professional hockey, or earn great plaudits in other aspects of their lives, but last evening's outcome will hang around their necks like an albatross for years and years to come

In a tournament like the one that concluded last night, a team doesn't WIN the Silver medal.

THE TEAM LOSES THE GOLD!

Granted, these young men are really just kids. Sometimes, kids do things that are regrettable, and the consequences are severe. Sometimes, the impact of their actions lasts for a very long time. That is something that will certainly ring true about last night's game.

In previous books that I have written, I have had occasion to publish the names of several Canadian Hockey teams who distinguished themselves by bringing honour and glory to Canada. No matter what accolades were awarded to individual players on this team, those recognitions hold little glory, even to the recipients, because the overall result was not GOLD.

Here, then, are the players and coaches who represented Canada in the 2010 – 2011 World Junior Hockey Tournament in Buffalo, New York, USA.

PLAYER	HOMETOWN	TEAM
GOAL		
Mark Visentin	Waterdown, Ontario	Niagara (OHL)
Olivier Roy	Causapscal, Quebec	Acadie-Bathurst (QMJHL)
DEFENCE		
Jared Cowan	Allan, Saskatchewan	Spokane (WHL)
Simon Despres	Laval, Quebec	Saint John (QMJHL)
Dylan Olsen	Calgary, Alberta	Minnesota-Duluth (NCAA)
Erik Gudbranson	Orleans, Ontario	Kingston (OHL)
Ryan Ellis	Freelton, Ontario	Windsor (OHL)
Tyson Barrie	Victoria, B.C.	Kelowna (WHL)
Calvin de Haan	Carp, Ontario	Oshawa (OHL)
FORWARDS		
Sean Couturier	Bathurst, N.B.	Drummondville (QMJHL)
Jaden Schwartz	Wilcox, Saskatchewan	Colorado College (NCAA)
Zack Kassian	LaSalle, Ontario	Windsor (OHL)
Brayden Schenn	Saskatoon, Saskatchewan	Brandon (WHL)
Casey Cizikas	Mississauga, Ontario	Miss.-St. Mikes (OHL)
Quinton Howden	Oak Bank, Manitoba	Moose Jaw (WHL)
Curtis Hamilton	Kelowna, B.C.	Saskatoon (WHL)
Marcus Foligno	Sudbury, Ontario	Sudbury (OHL)
Ryan Johansen	Port Moody, B.C.	Portland (WHL)

Louis Leblanc	Kirkland, Quebec	Montreal (QMJHL)
Cody Eakin	Winnipeg, Manitoba	Swift Current (WHL)
Carter Ashton	Saskatoon, Saskatchewan	Tri-City (WHL)
Brett Connolly	Prince George, B.C.	Prince George (WHL)

COACHES

Dave Cameron (HC)	Charlottetown, PEI	Miss.-St. Mikes (OHL)
Andre Tourigny	Nicolet, Quebec	Rouyn-Noranda (QMJHL)
Ryan Huska	Cranbrook, B.C.	Kelowna (WHL)
George Burnett	Port Perry, Ontario	Belleville (OHL)

Leafs Clip Blues with Shootout Win

For just a few minutes last night, I thought that the Maple Leafs were going to pull a repeat of the night before, and fold in the same manner as our Team Canada Juniors. Fortunately, that didn't happen. The Leafs were successful in earning both points that were up for grabs...and very badly needed.

The game was an odd one, to say the least. It started when the home team got on the scoreboard just fifteen seconds in, when Colby Armstrong deflected a shot into the net with his body. An early goal like that is obviously a morale booster for the team that scores, but the euphoria didn't last. St. Louis tied the game when Alex Steen, an ex-Leaf returning to the ACC for the first time since being traded away two years ago, scored his 14th goal of the current season. Before the first period was over, Steen's team-mate David Backes had potted his 11th.

The second period belonged to the home team. The boys went on a bit of a scoring rampage. Grabovski, Versteeg, and Kessel each scored in less than four minutes, and the hometown crowd roared their approval at this uncharacteristic power surge.

Early in the third stanza, Phil Kessel counted his second goal of the game, and the Leafs had a 5 to 2 lead. There was, at that point, every indication that victory was a pretty sure thing. How soon we forget!

Bang! Bang! Bang! What the heck is going on here??? Were we seeing a repeat of the night before, this time in Toronto rather than Buffalo??? Goals by Winchester, Brewer, and D'Agostini evened the score and quieted the crowd a bit.

Regulation time in this one ended with the score tied at 5 – 5. A five-minute overtime session solved nothing, so the shootout had to be the determinant for this night's winner. Eight different players got an opportunity to win the game for their respective teams, but the Blues could not match the Leafs. Two visitors scored, but three of the locals, Versteeg, Grabovski, and Bozak assured the Leafs of this important win.

The Leafs now embark on a four-game road trip that begins tonight in Atlanta. After the two weekend days off, they will play Monday in Los Angeles, Tuesday in San Jose, and Thursday in Phoenix. I see these games as critical in the overall scheme of things as the second half of the schedule is upon us.

Go, Leafs! Go!

The Jig is almost up!

Leafs on the Right End of a Blowout

This morning, if I had stepped outside my front door, and was greeted by my next-door neighbor, Pete, he might well have asked me, "What was the score of the Leafs' game last night?" Of course, my reply would have been, "9 to 3". Pete would have automatically assumed the worst, given the usual less than stellar performances that the Leafs have served up so far this season. This time, though, he would have been wrong!

The boys went on a real tear last night, and served up an old-fashioned Southern "whupping" to the Atlanta Thrashers right on their own ice.

At the 2:38 minute mark of the first period, Tobias Enstrom put the home team on the scoreboard. Immediately following that, Colton Orr and Erik Boulton dropped their gloves and engaged in a lively set-to, undoubtedly instigated by Orr to set a tone of belligerence among his mates. It worked. Before the end of the period, Versteeg and Grabovski had reclaimed the lead. The Leafs were ahead 2 to 1 at the first intermission.

In the first fifteen minutes of the second frame, the Leafs added to their lead with goals from Armstrong, Kulemin, and Grabovski. Then, at the 17:05 mark, there was a big rumpus in the corner of the Thrashers' zone. Dustin Byfuglien was penalized two minutes for roughing. Then, Ben Eager sucker-punched Colby Armstrong in the face. He was assessed a five-minute major, and expelled from the game.

In the five minutes that followed, (extending into the third period), the Leafs scored four more times. Those markers came off the sticks of Kulemin, MacArthur (2) and Kessel. **The Maple Leafs had scored EIGHT unanswered goals!** The home team had been humiliated by their guests.

The Leaf attack subsided as the final stanza of the game played out. The Thrashers scored two more goals, courtesy of Cormier and Ladd, but the game was completely out of reach. I have to admit that I thoroughly enjoyed this match, from start to finish.

Two wins in a row! The Leafs complete the first half of their schedule on Monday night when they take on the Los Angeles Kings on the west coast. They cannot let up. Another must-win has to be claimed or else the tire-spinning will continue. The Atlanta aberration was great for team morale, but can the momentum be sustained?

Go, Leafs! Go!

The Mastercard Centre for Hockey Excellence

The Toronto Maple Leafs and their AHL farm club, the Toronto Marlies, practice regularly at a wonderful new facility known as the Mastercard Centre for Hockey Excellence in Etobicoke. Located at 400 Kipling Avenue, this newly constructed complex houses FOUR NHL-sized (200' x 85') ice pads. One of the pads can be expanded to an Olympic-sized surface (200'x 100'). In addition to the ice surfaces, the Centre houses dressing rooms, training facilities, weight training rooms, and all other features required to keep the players fully trained and physically prepared to compete as professional athletes. In addition, the Centre is a marvelous community resource where hockey house leagues are conducted, and citizens from across the GTA can regularly visit for public skating sessions throughout the year. When fully complete, the Mastercard Centre will house offices of Hockey Canada, the NHLPA, and the Hockey Hall of Fame. It is indeed a unique place to visit.

Just a few days ago, my wife, Charlotte, and I journeyed from our home in Georgetown to attend a Maple Leaf practice at the Centre. It took approximately one hour to make the trip, and we arrived at our destination by 10:00 A.M. Our visit had been arranged by Pat Park, Director of Media Relations for the Leafs. We were greeted by a very courteous young lady who works at the Mastercard Centre. She gave us a brief explanation of the various features of the complex, and then took us upstairs on an elevator to a seating area that would comfortably accomodate a couple of hundred spectators. At one end of the rink, high above the ice, there are several images of the Stanley Cup, one for each championship won by past Leaf teams. A huge banner on the side opposite the seating area proclaims that this is the practice facility of the Toronto Maple Leafs. The Marlies have their own practice facilities directly across from the ones occupied by the parent club.

Every professional hockey team needs to have access to ice surfaces located separate and apart from their home arenas. The Air Canada Centre and the Ricoh Coliseum, the two home sites of the Leafs and Marlies, are both multi-purpose venues used to house and host concerts, exhibitions, fairs, and all manner of public gatherings that oblige the hockey operations to use other locations for their day-to-day functions. The Mastercard Centre allows the players space to have meetings, land-training facilities, rehabilitation capabilities, as well as on-ice practices. Access to the general public is able to be controlled.

The players arrive at the Centre at whatever time the practices are called for, and spend the first hour or more dealing with matters pertinent to their calling as professional athletes. There may be meetings with the coaching staff. There are warm-up exercises and activities that need to be carried out in preparation for a strenuous on-ice practice session. Then, the players must don their full equipment in preparation for the on-ice practice. As the first skaters emerge from the players' area, they scatter dozens of pucks onto the ice, and begin skating around and around, getting their "game-legs" under them.

Charlotte and I settled into our seats and waited for the team to appear. We were not alone. A couple of out-of-town hockey teams were also seated in the bleachers, eagerly awaiting the arrival of their heroes on the ice below. A television camera crew was also in the stands, undoubtedly assigned by their studio to get some film footage as the Leafs carried out their drills, and possibly set up an interview or two with specific players at some point.

Once all the players were assembled on the ice, the rink was literally a beehive of activity. The first thing that struck me was the reality that the players could not be easily identified. They did not have on their familiar jerseys...the ones with their names emblazoned on the back. Other than the three goalies, Giguere, Gustavsson, and Reimer. It was difficult to pick out specific players. Adding to the confusion, some of the players wore green jerseys, some wore red. All of the defencemen that day wore black.

We watched the practice for about an hour and a quarter. Believe me, those players worked hard all the time. Although the two of us were outsiders, and not intimately aware of how a professional hockey practice is orchestrated, it became clear that everything that was going on had specific purposes. There were several skating drills. There were stops and starts. There were line rushes. There were passing drills. At one time, the action proceeded up and down the entire length of the rink. Then the action went from one side to the other. There were shots taken at the goalies, and the rink echoed with loud "booms" as the pucks deflected off their pads. Every so often, a whistle blew, and the players gathered around one of the coaches for purposes of gaining instruction about one aspect of the game or another.

Most of us envision the life of professional hockey players as glamorous. They skate out onto the ice to the roar of their adoring fans. They are seen on television, and heard on the radio being interviewed about their game or their team-mates or their personal lives. All of them are required to appear throughout their home market at autograph sessions. Their photos are constantly seen in many magazines and publications.

All that is true, but, dear readers, you should also realize that these guys work for a living, just like you and me. They have to report for work almost every day at whatever time their bosses (a.k.a. coaches) specify. They exercise. They practice. They attend to their skates and sticks. They travel...sometimes thousands of kilometers from city to city in both the USA and Canada, from one side of the continent to the other.

I am grateful to Pat Park for allowing us to attend a Leaf practice. Our visit permitted us to see my favourite team in a setting far removed from the bright lights and hullabaloo of the Air Canada Centre. It was very interesting to get a brief glance into a less glamorous aspect of the working environment of a professional athlete.

Leafs Win Third Straight in Los Angeles

Jamie Reimer is looking more and more like he's the real deal. This young goalie, recalled from the Marlies when J. S. Giguere aggravated a groin injury a couple of weeks ago, has provided the Leafs with some excellent goaltending of late. Last night, he won his third consecutive game, coinciding with the efforts of his team-mates. Although it is too early yet to form any predictive judgments, it is certainly accurate to say that these good performances have materialized at a very opportune time.

The Leafs have now played exactly half of their regular 2010 – 2011 schedule. Over the next couple of days, I will compose and record my second team evaluation, and I'll conclude by giving my opinions about what the future needs to hold if the Leafs are to reach the post-season.

Last night's contest at the Staples Centre in Los Angeles was a very hard fought competition by both teams. The score is a true indication of how I felt the action unfolded.

Wayne Simmonds and Michal Handsus scored for the struggling Kings. They are currently playing a string of home games, and they have not been doing particularly well since Christmas. The Kings players are not yet overly concerned, but they recognize that they are going to need to get things turned around for themselves in the very near future. They played well last night, but were unable to gain any lasting advantage over the Leafs.

Following the game, Coach Ron Wilson was lavish in his praise of three of his recent recalls from the Marlies. Reimer, has been stalwart in the net for the blue and white. Darryl Boyce, who scored his second NHL goal in this one, is proving to be a gritty performer up front. Joey Crabb, who fed a beautiful pass to Phil Kessel for the second Leaf goal, has also made a very positive impression on the coaching staff.

The Leaf road trip continues this evening with another critical game in San Jose. The Leafs have not fared well over the years in this sun-drenched California city. It would be nice if they could turn their record here around tonight, especially given the urgent situation in which the Leafs find themselves. Following this game, the team will have a day off as they travel to Phoenix to meet the Coyotes on Thursday.

The pressure has been continuous on the Buds during the past couple of weeks. Every game is almost a case of "do, or die", and I think that the players are doing their best to respond to the need to do well on every shift that they play.

Four more points would give the Leafs a road trip that would do wonders to bolster their self-confidence and team morale.

Evaluation – The Leafs at Mid-Season

As is the case in all businesses of any consequence, evaluations are undertaken at key points in either the calendar or fiscal year in order to determine progress of the organizations towards their established goals. The Toronto Maple Leafs are no different in that regard. Their only important objective this season is to make the playoffs. That is the first step that MUST be achieved if any further success is to be realized.

The majority of Toronto media outlets have written off this year's version of the Toronto Maple Leafs.

<u>I have not!</u> Although I consider myself a legitimate writer, I am not a card-carrying reporter. I possess no media accreditations, and cannot claim any direct access to the players or club executives.

I am a fan! Nothing more…but nothing less! As a fan, I still believe that a playoff position this season remains attainable. However, I readily acknowledge that a supreme effort will have to be forthcoming during the second half of the schedule if the playoffs are to form a part of the Leafs' destiny at midnight on April 9, 2011.

The following is my detailed assessment of the current state of the Toronto Maple Leafs.

****

Overall

The Leafs have earned 38 points in the first half of the season. Their winning percentage is 46.3. Those figures explain why the team is regarded as a failure to this point in time. They stand 26th in the League…12th in the Eastern Conference…and 4th in the Northeast Division.

It will take a genuine resurgence to make the playoffs…**<u>but I believe that it is possible.</u>**

Goaltenders

The Leafs now have three goalies on the roster. Due to an aggravating groin injury suffered by J.S. Giguere, the team called up James Reimer from the Marlies. He has played very well during the time he has spent with the big club. When Giguere is ready to return to full service, Reimer will probably return to the farm club. His play bodes well for next season, when he will probably fulfill the role as the club's backup goalie.

Here is the goaltending record to date.

	Giguere	Gustavsson	Reimer
Game Appearances	18	22	6
Shots Against	455	596	188
Goals Against	47	63	10
Goal Against Average	2.9	3.1	1.9
Save Percentage	.89	.89	.94

In summary, I believe that all three goalies have performed well. Goaltending is not a problem for this team.

Defence

At the halfway point, I can sum up my opinion of the Leaf defence with a single word... **disappointing!**

The main, defining statistic of the defensive corps to date is **-13.** While the Leafs have scored 109 goals, they have had 122 scored against them. The team with the best defensive rating in the NHL is Vancouver...a commendable **+43.** The worst in the league is New Jersey, with a dreadful rating of **-55.**

In terms of production, that aspect of the work of the Leaf blueliners also ranks below expectations. Here are the statistics that tell the story:

	Goals	Assists	Points	+/-
Beauchemin	1	9	10	-3
Gunnarson	1	4	5	0
Kaberle	1	27	28	-1
Komisarek	1	7	8	-1
Phaneuf	1	6	7	-3
Lebda	0	1	1	-18
Schenn	2	7	**9**	**-2**
Totals	**7**	**61**	**68**	

If we return our attention to the league-leading Vancouver Canucks, we note that their offensive output is:

$$22 \quad + \quad 67 \quad = \quad 89.$$

The longest serving member of the Maple Leafs is Tomas Kaberle. Although he is regarded as the best player whom Burke can hold out as trade bait, he continues to maintain his insistence that he does not want to leave Toronto. Due to Phaneuf's injury in the first half, Kaberle's former assignment as Assistant Captain was returned to him, and he has retained that ranking since Phaneuf's return. His production is head and shoulders above the other defenders, and he continues to contribute well in terms of preventing goals.

Luke Schenn has continued to emerge from last year's "sophomore slump". He is maturing over time, and has not diminished the hopes of everyone that one day he will be the anchor of the Leafs' defence.

It is too early to assess Dion Phaneuf's performance as team captain. After so many years of great leadership by Mats Sundin, it would be grossly unfair to compare the two players. Phaneuf is a very young man, and it will take a lot of time to allow him to forge his own legacy. To date, there are some very positive indicators that I will write about elsewhere in this work. On the ice, he has struggled a bit in terms of his play, but we must acknowledge that the serious cut that he suffered early in the season probably impacted his ability to perform far more drastically than he allowed us to know.

Carl Gunnarsson continues to show a lot of promise for the future.

I honestly believe that Francois Beauchemin and Mike Komisarek are performing below not only MY expectation, but below their own. If those two players can find their true form, then the overall contribution of team defence to the team can be boosted to a level that can be deemed satisfactory, at least.

Forwards

As this is written, there are signs that the forward line combinations on the Leafs are starting to come together. As the first half of the season has ended, and the second half begun, the team has put together a four-game winning streak just like the one they opened with in October. While this development is encouraging, make no mistake…the Leafs have a very long way to go before they can be regarded as a playoff threat.

The team needs a power centre. They need a "horse" of a player who can provide some true impact on the team, particularly on Phil Kessel's line. To this point, Kessel has carried too much of a burden. He has tried to carry the team on his back, and that simply cannot be done. He has been frustrated on many occasions, because the goals have not been coming at the rate that has been expected. It is not Phil's fault. He is a sniper. He possesses superior shooting ability… remarkable hand-eye coordination. In order to make the most of Kessel's skills, he MUST have some reliable help in the form of a setup man (or two). Burke has repeatedly assured us that he is burning up the phone lines in attempts to find help, but the results thus far have not materialized.

The following data will serve to summarize the work of the Leaf forwards.

Centres

Eight players have suited up at centre ice for the Leafs this season. Four of them are currently assigned to the Marlies. The most promising of these four farmhands is Nazem Kadri. He was given a legitimate opportunity to make the jump from Junior to NHL in the first half of the schedule, but things just didn't work out. It became obvious that he just wasn't mature enough to adapt to life in the big leagues. Like so many…indeed MOST players, a period of maturation in the minor-pro ranks is required. The other three centres, Hanson, McKegg, and Zigomanis were not able to earn or hold a permanent roster spot

Here is the statistical story:

	Goals	Assists	Points
Grabovski	17	16	33
Bozak	7	10	17
Kadri	0	6	6
Mitchell	2	1	3
Brent	3	3	6
Zigomanis	0	1	1
Totals	**29**	**37**	**66**

To summarize, then, Mikhail Graabovski has emerged as a star for the team. He is a hard worker and a consistent point producer. Tyler Bozak is emerging as a confident, steady performer, and his future looks bright. John Mitchell has had a very disappointing year, and it is difficult to know the reason(s) for his less than stellar work production. Tim Brent is doing a stalwart job on special teams, and shows a lot of enthusiasm and loyalty. Numbers don't lie. **The need for a centre is urgent.**

Left Wing

Five players have patrolled the left side of the rink for this year's Leafs. One of them, Luca Caputi, has been unable to stick with the big club, and has therefore been sent back down to the Marlies. Of the remaining four, two are showing signs of becoming star players. Nikolai Kulemin displays a high skill level night after night. Clarke MacArthur, signed as a free agent after being rejected by the Atlanta Thrashers, has become a sniper possessed of scoring ability similar to his team-mate Kessel. Fredrik Sjostrom is doing yeoman work on the special teams, and young Darryl Boyce, recently promoted to the Leafs, is showing considerable promise. The following figures tell the story on left wing.

	Goals	Assists	Points
Kulemin	16	14	30
Boyce	2	2	4
Sjostrom	1	3	4
MacArthur	12	22	34
Totals	**31**	**41**	**72**

I believe that Ron Wilson and his staff are relatively satisfied with the performance of their left-wing skaters.

Right Wing

Few would argue that the Leafs are strongest on their right wing. A complement of six players share the responsibility for this position, and thus far they have acquitted themselves reasonably well. Mike Brown and Colton Orr are both tough competitors who sit patiently on the bench awaiting "spot duty" when called upon by Wilson and his staff. Orr is the team's "enforcer". Joey Crabb is yet another recent call-up from the Marlies, and he has made a very good first impression among his team-mates. Colby Armstrong, a feisty young player picked up in the off-season from Carolina, has had some significant injury problems that have limited his playing time, but he holds promise as an impact player if he can remain healthy. Kris Versteeg and Phil Kessel are both recognized as major contributors to any future Leaf success.

Here are the first-half stats for skaters on the right wing.

	Goals	Assists	Points
Brown	1	1	2
Kessel	18	12	30
Orr	2	0	2
Versteeg	12	19	31
Armstrong	5	5	10
Crabb	0	5	5
Totals	**38**	**42**	**80**

Summary

Admittedly, things aren't looking great at the halfway point in the schedule. Brian Burke wants his team to make the playoffs. He practically promised the Maple Leaf Nation that this year's club would achieve that goal. However, there is a very steep hill to climb if the objective is to be attained. Indeed, as I have said, the Toronto media have already written the Leafs off.

Several things need to happen if success is to be met this year:

1. Brian Burke MUST acquire an impact centre ice player.

2. Team defence MUST contribute more assistance in terms of point production to augment the work of the forward lines.

3. The forwards and defence combined must continue to develop their coordination and team chemistry to raise their goals-per-game average to a level of 3.5 at least.

4. Goaltending must remain a solid constant in order to support the Leaf skaters.

Leafs Get Win #600 for Coach Wilson

This morning, congratulations are certainly deserved by head coach Ron Wilson, who last night reached a landmark in his coaching career. Thanks to a good effort by the Leafs, the win marked the 600th victory for their coach. Ironically, this triumph came at the expense of the San Jose Sharks, the team that fired Wilson just three years ago. Even though the Toronto fans have been screaming lately for Wilson to be fired from his current position, it must be acknowledged that six hundred wins in the NHL is a significant achievement for any head coach.

The victory also was the Leafs' fourth in a row…matching the team's effort at the beginning of the season. It would be a great achievement if they could defeat the Coyotes on Thursday night, and allow them to skate out onto the ice at the ACC on Saturday boasting a very successful road trip. Let's hope!

It took the Leafs most of this game to get untracked. Patrick Marleau scored midway through the first period to give the home team the lead.

There was no scoring in the middle frame.

Phil Kessel got the Leafs on the scoreboard early in the third when he circled in front of the opposition net before patiently and accurately depositing the puck behind Niemi. Clarke MacArthur followed shortly thereafter, scoring a power-play goal.

Marleau then scored his second marker of the night to tie the score, and put his team back into the match. However, it was to be the Maple Leafs that would ultimately claim the two points on this occasion. Carl Gunnarson scored what would eventually be the winning goal, and Clarke MacArthur finished the match with a final-minute goal…his second of the game.

This game also featured some very good goaltending by Jamie Reimer in the Leaf net. He has been most impressive in the past few games, and may have even worked well enough to be given the start on Thursday, when the team winds up its current road trip. A fifth win by the club is almost too much to hope for. Still, they deserve full marks for the success that they have claimed in their last four outings.

Could this string of victories be the beginning of some sort of revival as the second half of the season begins? We'll have to wait and see. Still, we all know too well that some sort of a turnaround is desperately needed.

Let's keep our fingers crossed.

Leafs Close Road Trip with Head Shot Controversy

I am writing today's journal entry a bit later in the day than I normally do because the Leafs announced earlier that they were expecting the NHL to issue a suspension to tough forward Mike Brown. Sure enough, a few hours later the decision was handed down. Brown was suspended for three games for delivering a "head shot" to Ed Jovanoski of the Coyotes last night. More of that later.

The game was not well played by either team. Phoenix took the lead early in the first period with a goal by Radim Vrbata. There was no further scoring in either the first or second periods. The game was not a particularly entertaining one for the fans in the stands, or watching on television.

The Jovanoski – Brown incident happened late in the second. Although Brown maintains that he never meant to injure anyone, insisting that he was just playing his normal, robust game, it was an easy call for the league to make. At least three camera angles on the play clearly portray a purposefully delivered check by Brown, and a clear, hard contact to Jovanoski's head. In addition to the suspension, Brown's salary for the three games, more than $ 8,000, will be contributed to the Players' Emergency Assistance Fund.

Phoenix woke up, and responded vigorously to Jovanoski's injury in the third. They stepped up their attack and scored four goals. Markers by Doan, Pyatt, and Korpkoski gave the Coyotes a 4 – 0 lead before Colby Armstrong finally netted one for the Leafs. Keith Yandle potted his team's fifth goal with less than a minute to go in the contest.

This was a disappointing final game on what has been a very successful road trip for Toronto. Ten points out of ten would have been nice, but the team will have to settle for eight. Perhaps the Leafs can start another streak on Saturday night, when the Calgary Flames visit the ACC.

****

Head shots continue to be an on-going, major problem in the NHL. Tomorrow night, Sidney Crosby will miss his fifth game as the result of a head shot that he sustained in the Annual Outdoor Classic on January 1st. I am personally worried and dismayed that this issue is not going away. Injuries to the head are far too frequent in the game today. The league and the Players' Association need to do everything possible to reduce these situations before someone's career is ended...OR WORSE!

Another "No Horses Loss"

I am starting to get a little ticked off about one of Brian Burke's supposed beliefs about his Maple Leafs. I have heard him state, on more than one occasion that he felt the current roster made up a "competitive" team. **I beg to differ!**

The Leafs are NOT competitive with their present roster!

For gawd's sake, Brian…wake up and smell the coffee!

Take a couple of these guys out of the lineup and the production of the rest of them drops off to practically NOTHING. Last night, Versteeg couldn't play because of injury and Mike Brown was suspended. Result: the only Leaf able to score was good old reliable Grabovski with his 18th of the season…and it took him nineteen minutes and forty-seven seconds to do it!

Last night was the TENTH Leaf loss by a single goal. Six of those losses have been to clubs that, like the Leafs, do NOT currently hold a playoff spot. If the Leafs were truly competitive, they could have beaten those clubs and would be within range of the post-season right now. They aren't!

Over the past couple of years, I have noticed that a pattern can be detected when non-playoff teams pay visits to the Air Canada Centre. For some inexplicable reason, the Leafs frequently lose. Why should this be the case? I believe that this situation can be traced to what I call… "motivational deficit". Here is my explanation.

Every NHL club knows that Toronto is the centre of the hockey universe. Media coverage is huge. Most games are telecast at least across the province…and many across the whole country. Visiting players WANT to play better when they visit the Toronto market. All of their friends and family will be watching them. In other words, they are intrinsically EXTREMELY motivated to perform at a higher level than usual.

To the Leafs, on the other hand, it often appears that they regard the match as just another home game. They are used to all the hoopla…all the cameras…all the reporters. Their motivation level, therefore, needs to be _extrinsically_ boosted a bit. That, in my opinion, ids the responsibility of Ron Wilson and his staff…and on many occasions I believe that they have fallen short of that responsibility.

Mr. Burke …SOMETHING is wrong here! Your team lacks intrinsic motivation! Why can't the players get fired up to the point that they really "sock it to these weaker opponents" beginning in the first period? Are you really prepared to admit that **your guys just aren't good enough? What is YOUR theory about this? If I am right …what in Sam Hill are you going to do about it?**

Leafs Disgrace Themselves on Broadway

I just did a word count on my current book about the 2010 – 2011 Leaf season. It tells me that I have written 35, 376 words outlining the progress (or lack thereof) of this motley crew of hockey players.

Why?

Why am I sitting in front of my computer for at least an hour, almost every day, just to eventually wind up with a book that nobody will want to read?

Why bother writing a book that will never be published…and will just wind up sitting somewhere on a shelf gathering dust?

Right now…at this precise moment…I can't give you an answer.

After the absolutely pathetic and putrid effort that the Leafs served up in New York last night, I have decided that, for the next few days I am NOT going to use the "p" word…You know…the "p" word that has eight letters, and indicates the central objective of this year's team. For the time being, use of that word is not appropriate!

Yesterday, Kris Versteeg, slated to return to action after a minor injury, was quoted in the media as saying that the next five games will be the most critical and important of the Maple Leaf season. Then the team went out onto the ice at Madison Square Gardens and stunk out the joint.

Summary – These guys can talk the talk…but they can't walk the walk!

In light of last night's regrettable effort, today I have decided to simply unload, and put on paper several thoughts that are coursing through my mind lately. Maybe it will turn out to be a catharsis of some sort. Here goes!

Brian Burke   At the beginning of the season, you uttered public assurances that this year was going to be better…that you were tired of watching crappy hockey. Well, what do you call last night? It looked pretty crappy to me!

You're starting to look a little bit like Nero. You, know… he's the guy many years ago who fiddled while Rome burned to the ground around him.. Well, Brian…look around! Rome is burning! When are you and your management team going to stop fiddling around, and do something to put out the flames?

Ron Wilson Believe it or not, I do have a bit of sympathy for you when the ACC crowd starts to holler for your head on a platter. Such things shouldn't happen to a coach with six hundred wins under his belt. But, what have you (and your staff) done for the Leafs lately? Honestly, there have been some nights this season when I saw little or no evidence that your team had been properly prepared for a game. On MANY occasions, I could see very scant evidence that you and your confreres had taught the players any strategy to use in specific situations. You have been head coach now for almost three years. When are we going to see some acceptable results? Have you lost your edge? Is there a "generation gap" between you and your players? Are these guys just slow learners? **What's going on?????**

Some Team Questions and Comments

Goaltending

Jonas Gustavsson is NOT the goaltending future of the Leafs. He is NOT a MONSTER, so I wish that people would stop calling him that! My dog, Murphy, got a toy monster for Christmas. The toy is a cute little pink dragon with little blue wings, and a squeaker inside his tummy. We call him "Puff". That's what we should call Gustavsson. He hasn't been a monster since he left Sweden.

Jamie Reimer recently auditioned very well for a spot on the Leafs...but not right now! He should spend the remainder of the season down with the Marlies, where he can hone his skills and continue to build his confidence. Bringing him back to the parent club, considering their level of play, might destroy his career as a goalie, just like it has almost wiped out his buddy, Jonas.

Defence

Disappointing is a mild way of describing the work of this year's Leaf blueliners. Considering the amount of money that they are being paid, Burkie and the big boys in the organization are getting screwed...BIGTIME.

Luke Schenn is arguably the most promising of the lot...and he isn't even being paid a million dollars this year.

Beauchemin has yet to show that he has been worth the effort of bringing him to the Leafs. He has certainly not distinguished himself.

Is Mike Komisarek still trying to play with some sort of serious, but undisclosed injury...or is he really just as bad as he looks out there night after night?

Why is Kaberle still here in Toronto? It has been clear forever that Ron Wilson doesn't really want him on the team. For gawd's sake, he took the "A" away from him last summer, and only gave it back when Phaneuf got hurt. I don't understand why Kaberle even wants to play for Wilson...and some nights...HE DOESN'T!

Speaking of Phaneuf…why is this guy the Captain? Where is the on-ice leadership? He may be doing an acceptable job in his off-ice responsibilities, but game in and game out, he has been AWOL when his presence should count. He is a young man, and may have considerable promise, but things are not going well for him since he came to Toronto last year. **Trouble… thy name is Dion!**

The rest of the defenders are marginal, at best!

Forwards

Centre

The Leafs only have ONE centre who is worth a hoot. Grabovski! Bozak shows promise, but he lacks consistency.

What on earth is wrong with John Mitchell? He has THREE point in 45 games, and is still on the Leaf roster. What secret is being covered up in his case? Is he a drinker? Is he on drugs? Is he embroiled in some sort of major personal issue? The fans deserve some sort of accountability about him. What's going on?

Why is Mike Zigomanis wallowing in the AHL with the Marlies? He may not be deemed to be fast enough for the big club, but he has above average skills in winning face-offs. None of the Leafs do. This year, he has 7 goals and 20 assists with the Marlies, and I believe that he would be an improvement over some of the dead meat that currently plays for the Leafs.

Left Wing

Kulemin and MacArthur are the only left-wingers of any value to this team. Boyce is a comer. The other guys are barely worth a pail of pucks.

Right Wing

While right wing is the strongest element on the Leafs, I have some reservations about Phil Kessel? Is he really everything he's cracked up to be? Is he really the guy that Burke intends to build a cup-winner around. Some nights he shows some true brilliance, but on other nights, he looks and plays in a VERY ordinary way. In **NINETEEN** of the forty-five games this season, he has not produced a single point. In my opinion, he looks a little too pudgy to be classified as a superior athlete. He reminds me of the Pillsbury Dough Boy, who giggles when a big finger pokes him in the tummy. To his credit, he has tried on occasion to carry the team on his back, but we all know that NOBODY is good enough to do that!

Well…that's my rant! Tonight, the Leafs take on the Anaheim Ducks at the ACC. After last night's so called performance, they have a helluva lot to prove!

Rebound...NOT Recovery!

Well, the Leafs did last night what they pretty well HAD to do in light of their absolutely disgraceful performance in New York on Wednesday. It was a case of "all hands on deck" for this game. No slackers allowed!

As usual, the Leafs surrendered the first goal to the Ducks in the first, when Dan Sexton popped one behind J. S. Giguere, who was facing his former team at the ACC for the first time ever. Fortunately, Clarke MacArthur was able to tie the score later in the period.

Three goals were scored in the second frame. Brandon McMillan put Anaheim ahead for a short time, but the Leafs slammed the door on the visitors for the rest of the match. MacArthur made a great rush into the Anaheim zone, circled the net, and made a brilliant pass to Gunnarsson, who fired a blazing shot past Hiller. Then, Tyler Bozak scored with a beautiful shot into the enemy net, set up beautifully by Phaneuf and Kessel. That goal eventually proved to be the winner.

The third period belonged, deservedly so, to Mikhail Grabovski. The speedy little centre scored twice...both goals on backhands. The first goal was unassisted, and the second was set up by his line mate MacArthur, whose assist was his third point of the night (one goal and two helpers). The final goal of the game was the 20th marker of the season for Grabovski, whose consistent efforts are being rewarded so far this season.

Prior to this game, there was a lot of media talk about changes to the Leafs...especially in light of last Wednesday's train wreck at MSG in New York. Several names were bandied about. One comment suggested that there would not be many "untouchables" on the Leaf roster. I would suggest, though, that there are some. Here are the players that I would identify as untouchable, and deserving of a contract if they don't already have one.

Goal	**James Reimer**		
Defence	**Dion Phaneuf**	**Carl Gunnarsson**	**Luke Schenn**
Forwards	**Tyler Bozak**	**Mikhail Grabovski**	**Nik Kulemin**
	Darryl Boyce	**Clarke MacArthur**	**Kris Versteeg**
	Phil Kessel	**Colby Armstrong**	**Joey Crabb**

All of those not included in the list above are expendable. I believe that the thirteen players that I have identified as keepers can form the core of a really good team.

Ovechkin Feasts on Valiant Leafs

It would be totally unfair to level much criticism at the Maple Leafs over last night's loss to the Capitals. This was a very entertaining game...fast-paced, and the Leafs kept the score close for most of it. Let's face it, readers, did we <u>really</u> expect a Leaf victory? Washington stands FIFTH in the Eastern Conference, while the Leafs occupy TWELFTH place.

In my humble opinion, there were three factors that contributed to the Capitals' victory in this contest:
1. A strong defensive effort by the visitors
2. A hot goalie - Holtby
3. Alex Ovechkin.

We were treated last evening to see Alex Ovechkin at the top of his game. Without question, he is one of the best players in the league. There are few players who can match his zeal for playing offensive hockey. Few want the puck more than he does. His speed, when he puts the pedal to the metal, resembles an afterburner on a jet plane. That was exemplified last night on his last goal, when he blazed past Tomas Kaberle, cut sharply in front of Dion Phaneuf, and deposited the puck in an empty net.

Ovechkin doesn't give a rat's patootie whether he counts a goal or an assist. As long as the puck hits the back of the net, he celebrates as exuberantly as one can imagine. Nobody on his team wants to win more than he does. Over the years, Toronto is one of the clubs that he has feasted upon. His hat trick last night served to keep the tradition rolling.

We haven't heard a lot from Brian Burke this week. He was at this game, watching intently from his lofty position high above the ice. He has probably felt a little better about his team and their much improved play since the slaughter in New York, but I am certain that he realizes that the players, for the most part, have let him down this year. With the trade deadline fast approaching, he and his managerial assistants have a lot of work to do. As I indicated in my most recent journal entry, I believe that there is a core element of a good team in place, but, at the same time, some MAJOR decisions must be made in the near future.

I do not envy him as he enters a critical phase of his term as General Manager. The impact of his next few weeks in charge of the franchise will be critical...to say the least!

Yet Another Wasted Opportunity

Speaking to the media following Carolina's defeat of his team last night, Captain Dion Phaneuf stated that this was a very disappointing loss. What else is new? I sense that a cloud of disappointment has enveloped the Leafs ever since they returned from their successful road trip out west. At the end of that trip, during which they won four of the five games that they played, their winning percentage was 47.6. With just two or three more wins, they could have brought their record over the 50% mark, and given themselves a genuine boost in team confidence and morale. They would have positioned themselves for a real battle down the home stretch.

Sadly, they couldn't do it!

Six games played…FIVE LOSSES! Winning percentage…back to 44.7!

This season's trade deadline is February 28th, at 3:00 P.M. There have been rumblings in the Toronto media that changes are coming. The players all know that this team has fallen short of expectations, and I believe that most of them are just waiting for the shoe to drop. Brian Burke may act at any time now, or he may wait until the deadline day. With the All-Star break happening this coming weekend in Raleigh, he may well have an opportunity to pull the trigger on some sort of deal. Clearly, for fans and players alike, we are immersed in a waiting game.

Young Tim Brent had a career game last night, chalking up two goals and an assist. Good for him! The Leafs kept things close for most of the game. The score was tied 3 – 3 until almost halfway through the third, and the boys had a chance to "make some hay."
Then, things broke the other way. Two quick goals by Sutter and Skinner put the home team out in front, and Toronto just didn't have enough juice to catch up. A late goal by Mike Brown got them close again, but the "coup de grace" was administered by Erik Cole in the final minute of play. Seven goals made for a wild third period.

Tonight, Jamie Reimer has been recalled from the Marlies to start this game against the Lightning, in Tampa Bay. With Gustavsson's confidence at a low ebb, it will be interesting to see what happens with Reimer acting as the final line of defence. The game is not particularly critical in terms of its importance. Most of the players are probably looking forward to a couple of days off with their families.

At one time, a few moons ago, this team got us all off to what looked like there might be some sort of revival ahead for this moribund franchise. Oh, how things have changed since then. A huge chunk of excitement and anticipation has disappeared into thin air. Again…we wait… and wait…and wait!

Nothing to Report from Tampa Bay

Another "nothing" night for the Toronto Maple Leafs! My personal expectations were not high going into this game. I could see very little chance that they could claim a victory. After all, they had played the night before, and that fact alone would negatively mitigate their chances against their well-rested opponent.

In terms of personnel, the Lightning had it all over the Leafs like a tent. Tampa Bay boasts two of the top scorers in the NHL on their roster. Steven Stamkos is the top scorer in the league as this is written. He has 38 goals and 29 assists, for a total of 67 points. Not far behind him is his team-mate Martin St. Louis with 20 goals and 40 assists. The top scorer on the Leafs, Clarke MacArthur, has 40 points. Enough said!

As far as league standings are concerned, Tampa Bay occupies THIRD place, while Toronto is TWENTY-SIXTH.

Those are the facts, dear readers!

This situation must be driving Brian Burke absolutely NUTS!

There are TWO positive things that I can say about the Leafs last night. They did play a decent game. The rather close score indicates that they DID compete in the contest. It is also appropriate to Commend Jamie Reimer, who played in the Leaf net, for his fine effort. He continued to play well in support of his struggling team-mates. His work for the Leafs since being called up a few weeks ago bodes well for the Leafs in the future.

There are no more games for the Leafs until next Tuesday, when the Florida Panthers will pay a visit to the ACC. I will be particularly interested in that game, because a young acquaintance of mine, Shawn Matthias, will be playing at centre ice for the visitors.

There are just 33 games remaining in the regular NHL season for the Leafs. With each mounting loss, hope for a successful season diminishes. A surge of wins would be nice to contemplate, but this year's current rate of success would suggest that the team is just not equipped to pull such a thing off. The math just doesn't look good.

The Key Maple Leaf Hopes for 2011 – 2012

Player # 1 – Phil Kessel

Phil Kessel will be the cornerstone of next year's Maple Leaf team.

The Key Maple Leaf Hopes for 2011 – 2012

Player # 2 – Dion Phaneuf

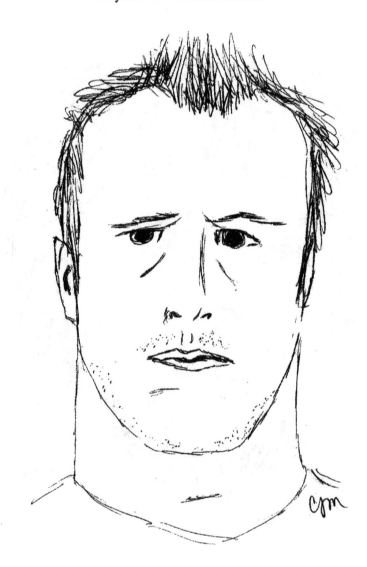

Dion Phaneuf will be counted upon for his leadership as team Captain.

The Key Maple Leaf Hopes for 2011 – 2012

Player # 3 - James Reimer

James Reimer has laid claim to the role of starting goaltender in 2011 – 2012.

The Key Maple Leaf Hopes for 2011 – 2012

Player # 4 – Luke Schenn

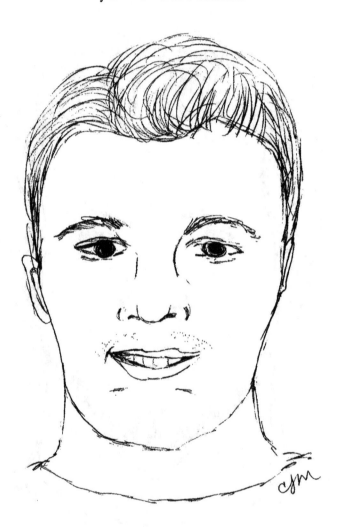

Luke Schenn is fast becoming one of the NHL's premier defencemen.

The Key Maple Leaf Hopes for 2011 – 2012

Player # 5 – Nikolai Kulemin

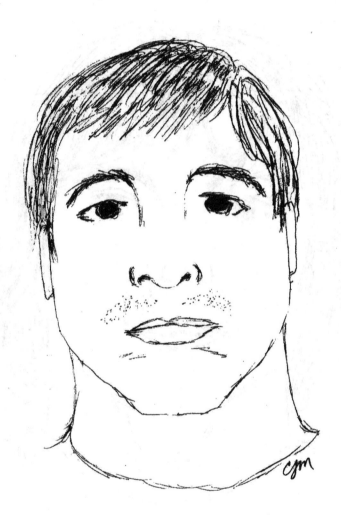

Nikolai Kulemin shows great potential as one of the Leafs' steadier scoring threats.

The Key Maple Leaf Hopes for 2011 – 2012

Player # 6 – Mikhail Grabovski

Mikhail Grabovski combines speed with explosive scoring capability.

Leafs Nip Panthers in a Shootout

With their victory over the Panthers in last night's shootout, the Maple Leafs achieved a win percentage of 45. As a former Elementary School Principal, I can attest to one and all that 45 percent is NOT a passing grade. To be blunt, it is indeed a FAILING mark in anybody's book, and that is the reality that this team has to confront with just 32 games remaining in their regular season schedule.

Every player…to a man…knows that this year's club has failed to achieve the expectations that we all placed upon them at the beginning of October. Still, they will all tell you to your face that they still have a chance to make the post-season. The vast majority of both their fan base AND the media have already written the Leafs off, and indeed there is a great deal of speculation about possible personnel changes as the trade deadline (February 28 – 3:00 P.M.) approaches.

The Leaf players have locked in to the idea of approaching each game individually…one game at a time. They want to climb upwards in the standings two points at a time. **Single point efforts will NOT get the job done!** Two…by two…by two…by two! **They are determined to put themselves into a competitive position this season, and they are convinced that they can do so in the next two months. <u>There are no white flags in the proximity of the Leaf clubhouse.</u>**

Last night was their first success. You could sense their relief as the team clamored over the boards immediately following J.S. Giguere's final shootout save against Chris Higgins of the Panthers. Two points down…a whole bunch more to go!

The game itself was a hard-fought affair. For once, Toronto opened the scoring, when Kris Versteeg bounced the puck into the net off Clemmensen's derriere. Weiss tied the game with his 14th of the season, and then Kulemin put the Leafs out in front with his 17th marker this year.

The teams each scored once in the middle frame. First, it was Booth for the Panthers, and then Grabovski put the Leafs ahead with his 21st goal in a very successful season.

The third period saw the Panthers outshoot the Leafs by a margin of 12 to six, and they were rewarded for their strong effort when Cory Stillman beat Giguere for the tying goal. Regulation time ended with the teams deadlocked. Overtime did not result in a winner, therefore the shootout followed. Tyler Bozak and Colby Armstrong scored for Toronto, but only David Booth was able to beat the steady Giguere.

Tomorrow night, the Leafs face their next tough challenge when Carolina pays another visit to the ACC. Another brace of points is BADLY needed.

Reimer Delivers Leaf Victory with First NHL Shutout

Congratulations today to Jamie Reimer, who backstopped the Leafs to an impressive victory over the Carolina Hurricanes at the ACC last night. It is clear that Reimer is enjoying his time with the big club. He is right on top of his game. Last night, I was particularly impressed with the way that he was controlling any rebounds. He was clearly making certain that there was no opportunity for the opposition to jump on a loose puck and pop it behind him.

Kudos also to young Tim Brent, who put on an absolutely heroic show midway through the game. He blocked three or four shots in a row when the Leafs were short-handed, and his efforts were unanimously applauded by his team-mates.

There was no scoring in the first period of this game. Toronto outshot the visitors by a margin of 13 to 6, but All-star goalie Cam Ward was impressive with his stalwart work in the net. I was a bit concerned that in the final analysis it would be the veteran, Ward, who would prevail over the rookie, Reimer. However, I need not have been worried. Reimer's confident effort, along with steady play by the home team, tipped the scales in favour of the blue and white.

In the second frame, Clarke MacArthur notched his 16th goal of the season to open the scoring. Later in the period, Darryl Boyce blistered down the right wing past a Carolina defender, cut toward the net, and fired a hard shot past Ward. Early in the third, Kris Versteeg scored with a beautiful wrist shot just a few seconds after Ward had made a brilliant save to thwart a Leaf attack. From that point on, the steady defence played by the home team held their visitors off the score sheet, and Reimer got the very first shutout of his career.

At the beginning of the season, it was generally felt that the Leaf goaltending situation was stable. Giguere, the elder of the two goalies, would be designated the primary role in the net. He would mentor Gustavsson, who would fulfill the back-up position. Things have not evolved according to that plan. Giguere missed several games due to a groin issue. Gustavsson struggled, one game after another, and over time, his self-confidence eroded. There was also some speculation that his team-mates lost some confidence in his work. That resulted in Reimer being called up from the Marlies, and his work in the big league has impressed everyone. It was announced just the other day, that Gustavsson has been sent down the AHL Marlies for a one-week conditioning stint.

Next up for the Leafs will be a Saturday bus ride down the QEW to Buffalo. The team, in recent years, has a rather unfortunate history when paying visits to their closest NHL neighbours. This Saturday MUST yield a different, and POSITIVE result. I have a good feeling about this game. Let's see if it bears out!

Another Slaughter at the HSBC Abattoir

The Maple Leafs took a bus trip to Buffalo yesterday. When they crossed the border into the USA, they were asked the customary questions by the authorities… "Where were they going?" and "Why are you going there?" Of course, they answered that they were going to Buffalo to play hockey against the Sabres.

Well, that WAS their intent. It wasn't EXACTLY what happened.

At the border stop on their way home, the Leafs were asked if they had anything to declare. They answered in the negative. They were bringing nothing back. The way they played might suggest that they didn't take much over the border in the first place. I said the other day that I had a good feeling about the possible outcome of last night's game. I must have been running a fever, or something. I should have known better. The Leafs haven't beaten the Sabres in Buffalo since December, 2008.

This game was just plain ugly. The score was 2 – 0 before the six-minute mark of the first period. Goals by Pominville and Stafford put the home team ahead. Jamie Reimer wasn't to blame for those goals. His team-mates couldn't get their feet moving. Play was concentrated in the Leaf defensive zone for most of the period.

Buffalo scored three goals in the second period, and the television commentators reported over and over again that the Sabres were in total control of the game. Sabre marksmen were Gaustad, Connolly, and Stafford, with his second of the night. Nik Kulemin stuffed a puck past Miller to get the Leafs on the board.

The teams traded goals in the third, with Beauchemin's second marker of the season, followed by Vanek's 19th. I watched the game right until the bitter end, hoping all the time for some sort of comeback effort, but none was forthcoming.

If there is a player on the Leafs that I have genuine concerns about, that player is Phil Kessel. He is working very hard, but is realizing ZERO results. Both last night and the previous game against Carolina, he had breakaways on the opposing goalie, but was thwarted both times. His frustration is palpable. Television shots from both of the most recent Leaf outings have shown Kessel sitting on the bench after extreme efforts, gasping from exhaustion and shaking his head in frustrated disbelief. The stress on this young man is immense, and I worry that he may not be able to handle it much longer. A great deal is expected of him, and thus far he has not been able to deliver.

On Monday, the Leafs entertain the Atlanta Thrashers, then travel to New York to play the Islanders on Tuesday. With exactly thirty games left in the schedule, a winning streak of significant proportion is necessary. There mustn't be any more shoddy performances like the one last night. The jig is almost up!

My Concern Intensifies to ALARM!

Yesterday was Super Bowl Sunday. Although I am not a close follower of the NFL, I can claim that I do keep myself aware of what is going on in pretty well every major sporting endeavor. Consequently, I was sitting comfortably in my living room, watching my HDTV screen as the Packers and the Steelers fought it out for the Lombardi Trophy. (Green Bay Won)

At one point, I pulled out my i-phone, and called up the TSN app, just to review what else might be going on in the wide world of sports. One of the headlines piqued my curiosity. It read, "**Reflective Moment".** I called up the story and read it in its entirety. The contents of the article shocked me to my bootstraps!

This was a story about Phil Kessel, and it was written by a TSN staffer following Saturday night's Leaf defeat at the hands of the Buffalo Sabres. The article elaborated upon the very concern that I wrote about just yesterday in this journal. It told of Kessel's frustration about his on-going scoring slump. It related that Head coach Ron Wilson had benched him for part of Saturday's game, and then demoted him to the team's third line.

Here are some of Kessel's exact words, as quoted in the article:

When asked if Wilson had ever pulled him aside to talk about any issues, Kessel said, **"No, me and Ron don't really talk. That's all I have to say about that."**

At another point, Kessel alluded to his current scoring slump, which has now reached ten games. He said, **"I don't really know what to say about that any more. I'm trying. Obviously it's not going right. It might not be working out here. What are you going to do?"**

Kessel's final statement, like those outlined above, revealed his puzzlement and discouragement at the present state of affairs. **"I don't know. Maybe it's just not working out, I guess. Who know? I didn't get anything going. Maybe it's time for a change or something. Who knows?"**

In my opinion, all of the quoted words of this young Maple Leaf player serve to support the concern that I expressed in yesterday's journal entry. However, I submit that they also indicate that there are problems involving Kessel and Wilson that run much deeper than we have known before.

Phil Kessel is 23 years old! He is just a kid, in terms of his potential NHL career! **HIS COACH IS NOT COACHING HIM! HIS COACH IS NOT EVEN COMMUNICATING WITH HIM!**

It looks and sounds to me like the Kessel situation is nearing some kind of breaking point. Kessel is obviously very, very discouraged. Is he suggesting that things are going so poorly for him in Toronto that maybe he could do better somewhere else? What is he talking about when he mentions "maybe it's time for a change, or something"?

Well readers…if there's going to be any changes made, I would like to suggest to you, and to Brian Burke, and to anyone else willing to listen, that the most necessary change on the horizon involves Ron Wilson and his coaching staff.

I have said it before…and I'll say it again. The time has come for Brian Burke to make a coaching change. Phil Kessel's words, quoted in yesterday's TSN interview has confirmed in my mind the fact that Wilson's coaching style is no longer being effective. If he is not coaching Kessel…or even talking to him…what does that suggest is the case with the other young players on the team? Over the past couple of years there have been SEVERAL instances when I felt that the entire team had not been properly prepared to play certain, specific opponents.

Phil Kessel's words, yesterday, strongly suggest to me that there is an UNBRIDGABLE generation gap between Wilson and his young players, and I would go even farther, and suggest that several of his VETERAN players have stopped listening to him.

Brian Burke hasn't said much in the media of late. His silence is starting to scream at me. Where was he on Saturday night? Cliff Fletcher and Dave Nonis were at the Buffalo game. Where was Burke? When is he going to face up to the growing crisis that is unfolding right under his nose?

Even though I have not yet conceded that this season is a write-off, there are many people, both in the media and elsewhere, who have! With the trade deadline approaching, it appears that several Leaf players may finish the season sporting different colours than they currently wear. When those players reach their new destinations, will we then…and only then find out what was really going on back in Toronto? Will it be weeks…or months…or even years before we get the real story about the trials and tribulations of the Leafs during the Wilson years?

Come on, Brian! Make the coaching change! Promote Dallas Eakins! Give a younger guy the opportunity to evoke the changes that are going to be needed to transform the Leafs into a challenger!

It is my considered opinion that Ron Wilson is not going to take the Leafs anywhere even close to the Stanley Cup! It's time for him to move on!

Leafs Rebound to Nip Struggling Thrashers

Congratulations to the Maple Leafs this morning for their comeback win over the Thrashers at the ACC last night. This game was played on the heels of the Kessel – Wilson controversy, and I will have more to say about that issue later. Needless to say, all eyes were on Kessel last night, and his frustrations continued. He failed to get a single point. His scoring drought has now extended to eleven games.

To the surprise of almost nobody, the Leafs surrendered the first two goals of the game, and were faced with the prospect of having to dig their way out of another deep hole. Kane and Byfuglien had given Atlanta the lead with their first-period goals. The Thrashers had utterly dominated the Leafs in that period, leveling a total of 18 shots at Giguere in the Toronto net. In that period, the referees assessed SIX penalties to the home team, and if "Giggy" had not been on top of his game, the results could have been devastating.

The tide began to turn in the middle frame. First, Dion Phaneuf scored his very first home-ice goal as a Maple Leaf with a slapper from high in the slot. Then, Grabovski tied the score with his 22nd goal of the season. Former Leaf Nik Antropov scored for the visitors to put them ahead, but then Clarke MacArthur tied the game at 3 -3.

The third period was hard-fought, but the Maple Leafs prevailed. Nik Kulemin pounced on a Byfuglien giveaway, and ripped an unassisted backhander behind the Atlanta goalie, and a few minutes later, Tim Brent scored to put the Leafs ahead. Andrew Ladd scored a final goal for the Thrashers, but they couldn't tie the score in the dying minutes of the game.

Tonight, the Leafs play their second game in a very busy week when they skate out to face the New York Islanders. We all know how badly the team needs points, so it will be interesting to see how well they can play on consecutive nights, this time with Jamie Reimer in their net. Let's hope for the best!

****

Yesterday, Brian Burke intervened in the Kessel – Wilson "dispute". He asked both parties to sit down and iron out their differences. Apparently, Kessel and Wilson followed their boss's orders. Problem solved…RIGHT?

WRONG!

Nobody in the media, or among true Toronto Maple Leaf fans should be under any illusions about this problem or any of the other issues with which this hockey club is contending. The team is in crisis mode, and I cannot help thinking that some dramatic new developments will be forthcoming **in the very near future.**

Lesser Lights Power Leafs Over Islanders

The difference in the scoring between the Leafs and the Islanders last night was two goals… in favour of the blue and white. I am rather happy to report that two players whose names rarely appear on the score sheet lit up the red light behind the opposition net on this occasion. Jay Rosehill, whose role is mainly that of a "tough guy" scored his first goal of the season, assisted by Luke Schenn. Fred Sjostrom, another player known more for his skills as a checker, notched his second.

Those two goals, augmented by a three-assist performance by young Darryl Boyce, propelled the Leafs past the Islanders for their second consecutive victory, and their fourth win in five games. The other Leaf scorers were Colby Armstrong, Tomas Kaberle, and Nik Kulemin.

This game started with a very unusual situation involving the New York goaltender. The Islanders' backup goalie, Kevin Poulin, was slated to start the game. Part way through the pre-game warm-up, he caught his skate in a rut, and fell to the ice, twisting his left knee in the process. He had to be helped to the dressing room, and was unable to play. This forced their emergency call-up, Mikko Kostinen, to replace Poulin in the net. It was Kostinen's very first NHL game. In all likelihood, he could hardly believe what was happening. Nobody could blame him when he was beaten by the first couple of shots directed his way by Armstrong and Rosehill.

Kostinen did settle down as the game progressed. And markers by his team-mates Moulson and Grabner tied the score by the end of the second period.

Three unanswered goals in the third period by Kaberle, Kulemin and Sjostrom put the Leafs into the lead by what proved to be a decisive margin. A late Islander goal off the stick of Rob Schremp pulled the home team within two.

The Leafs really needed these two points, picked up at the expense of an Islander team that is having a very unfortunate season. That same situation will be repeated on Thursday evening when the New Jertsey Devils visit the ACC. They, too, have struggled this year, and I hope that the Leafs will not let up. They have reached the point in their own struggles when every single point lost is tantamount to another nail in their coffin. The game on Thursday will be the third critical venture in a very busy, but important segment of the schedule.

Go, Leafs…GO!

The Winds of Change Begin to Blow

Brian Burke held a media conference yesterday, and on that occasion he wasted little time in announcing his first moves in re-arranging the roster of his moribund hockey team.

He had traded defenceman Francois Beauchemin back to the Anaheim Ducks, the team that Beauchemin had left as a free agent in the summer of 2009 to sign with the Leafs. Burke thanked Beauchemin for his service with the Leafs, commenting that the native of Sorel, Quebec had brought character and integrity to the Leafs. In terms of production he scored 7 goals and 36 assists as a Leaf blueliner.

In return, Blake acquired the services of forward Joffrey Lupul, who will join the club immediately, and will suit up tonight when the Leafs take on the New Jersey Devils, providing, of course, he passes a required medical examination.

Burke also acquired the rights to a 20-year-old defenceman named Jake Gardiner, who is currently playing hockey with the University of Wisconsin. This being the case, he will probably retain the status of "promising defensive prospect" for the foreseeable future.

The third element of the transaction was the Leafs receiving a conditional pick in the 4th round of the 2013 NHL Entry Draft.

Joffrey Lupul is 27 years old, and has played in the NHL for a little more than six seasons. In 395 NHL games, he has scored 112 goals, and assisted on 113 others, for a points total of 225. Lupul sees himself as a good two-way player. He has sustained serious back injuries while playing in Anaheim, and missed a great deal of playing time. He is still required to take antibiotics as part of his recovery from a severe post-surgery infection. He claims to be in good health, and is looking forward to playing in Toronto. He sees his new team as providing him with an opportunity to regain his skills, and help the Leafs as they fight to get back into the playoff picture.

Lupul will wear #19 as he takes to the ice as a Maple Leaf this evening. Of course, we all wish him luck with his new team, and hope that he can help to inspire them to victory.

This trade has resulted in the Leafs becoming an even younger team. In exchange for Beauchemin, a veteran aged 30, the Leafs gain Lupul, 27, and Gardiner, 20. I cannot help but think that there will be other changes coming down the pike in the next couple of weeks. Stay tuned!

The Bad Hockey Gods Do It Again!

Many years ago, there was a very popular television show called "Laugh In". Periodically, the stars of that show, Dan Rowan and Dick Martin, presented a trophy that they called "The Fickle Finger of Fate" award. If that award still existed, last night's winner would have been James Reimer.

Reimer was the goalie for the Toronto Maple Leafs yesterday evening as they played a very close and hard-fought battle with the lowly New Jersey Devils, a team that, believe it or not, is having a crappier season than the Leafs. Both Reimer and his Devil counterpart, Johan Hedberg, had played exceptionally well in their respective nets. In fact, after the dust had settled, both goalies were chosen as stars of the game.

Both teams were within 24 seconds of an overtime deadlock when Ilya Kovalchuk, a brilliant NHL marksman, blistered a wrist shot past Reimer, thereby claiming two points for his struggling team, while the Leafs skated away with just one.

In modern nomenclature, we would just comment that the mean-spirited Gods of Hockey had struck again. Rowan and Martin would have presented the Fickle Finger of Fate Award to Jamie Reimer. The poor kid deserved better!

Last night's win by the Devils was also important in that it was the 600th victory for the Devils' head coach, Jacques Lemaire. The venerable bench boss has been a fixture in the NHL for several decades now, both as a coach and an extremely skilled player.

As to the game itself, it should be noted that Joffrey Lupul made his debut in a Leaf uniform. He played a good, steady game, as did young Keith Aulie, recalled from the Marlies to replace the recently departed Francois Beauchemin. Phil Kessel's scoring drought continued, but he did work hard to assist on his team's only goal off the stick of Nik Kulemin. Grabovski also picked up a helper on that goal. New Jersey's only score in regulation time came from Danius Zubrus.

By picking up a single point, this outing was not a total loss for the home team. They now have a day off before travelling to Montreal for a "Hockey Day in Canada" tilt with the Canadiens. If they play with a bit of spit and vinegar tomorrow night, who knows, they might begin to look like they are still fighting for a spot in the post-season.

Ooooooops! I'd better stop talking like that! I don't want to jinx anybody…especially if they sport blue and white hockey uniforms!

Leafs Can't Match Habs at the Bell Centre

Other than showing up at the rink last night, the Maple Leafs didn't bring much to yesterday's "Hockey Day in Canada" match-up at the Bell Centre in Montreal. All night long, it was painfully clear that they were playing as individuals, and not as a team. This criticism applied to their work both when on the attack and in their own defensive zone. Absolutely no blame for this loss should fall upon the shoulders of J. S. Giguere in the Toronto net. He was solid throughout the game, and the score could have been embarrassing had he not played as well as he did.

As I sat in my living room watching the game, I could see clearly that the Leafs were trying... but they were just not getting anything done. Time after time, they were able to get the puck into the Montreal defensive zone, but they were stymied by either the tight play of the Hab blue liners or the steady, dependable efforts of Carey Price in the net. As the game progressed, I tried to put my finger on the specific reasons behind the feeble attack of the Leafs. I identified TWO factors that emerged by the end of the contest...age and a lack of team cohesiveness.

The Leafs are one of the youngest teams in the NHL. This is a reality that we tend to forget until developments on the ice oblige us to recognize it. Last night, Darryl Boyce stood out as an example of a young hockey player playing an undisciplined style of hockey that veteran players rarely do. Although he is 26 years old, and should know better, he was assessed THREE minor penalties in the third period alone...once for hooking, another time for tripping, and finally for cross-checking. The first of those three infractions resulted in a Montreal power-play goal, their final marker of the game, and that score more or less sealed the win for the home team. Undisciplined play is one hallmark of a young, immature bunch of players.

From the very beginning of the season, I have listened to many, many interviews on radio and television during which the players did their best to convince their audience that they regard themselves as a team. The trouble is that they don't play like a team. When they win, everything is sweetness and light. They hoot and holler. They leap into mass group hugs when the goals are scored. They bonk their helmeted heads together at the conclusion of a winning effort. And of course, in their interviews they talk the good talk.

But why do they lose so often? It seems clear to me that the skaters have lost confidence in Jonas Gustavsson. His diminished success, to me, reveals that his faith in the team-mates in front of him has also declined since October. This year's Leafs have just one forward line combination that has clicked consistently. (Grabovski - MacArthur – Kulemin) Everyone else appears to function as individuals. Finally, the offence and the defence have performed as separate and distinct entities. Sadly, the end product of all this is the dysfunctional team that we saw visiting the Bell Centre last night.

February 15, 2011

Burke Pulls the Trigger on Another Deal

Another Toronto Maple Leaf player has been sent packing to the greener fields of Philadelphia, P.A. Late yesterday, Kris Versteeg quickly packed his bags, said a few goodbyes, and headed to the airport. His destination was Tampa Bay, where tonight, he and his new team, the Flyers, take on the Lightning. In return for Versteeg, the Flyers gave Brian Burke a first round pick and a third round pick in this year's entry draft.

Last week, it was Francois Beauchemin who gratefully accepted his departure ticket and took a return flight back to sunny Anaheim, California. Coming this way was Joffrey Lupul, a promising young player who is slowly, over the last two games, becoming familiar with his new surroundings in Toronto.

In paying tribute to Kris Versteeg, Burke described him as a "good guy" but implied that he just didn't appear to be a good fit in Toronto. He wished him well with the Flyers, who currently are established as one of the top teams in the NHL. The Leaf GM also hinted in his media remarks that they are already working on at least one more deal to try and acquire a forward who would be capable of adding some more punch to what has been a mediocre offence to this point in the season.

With Beauchemin and Versteeg gone, the Maple Leafs still have the player that, in my opinion, is the most valuable trade-bait asset with the deadline less than a fortnight away. Tomas Kaberle SHOULD be on the move soon. If Burke cannot move him by the deadline, the Leafs will, in all likelihood, watch him walk away in July to the team of his choice as a free agent, and receive NOTHING in return. If that happens, it will undoubtedly be viewed by the media as a major failure of the Burke regime at the ACC.

Brian Burke made a point of saying yesterday that he and the team still have their eyes set upon the final playoff spot in the Eastern Conference. That certainly is an admirable objective, but, let's face reality…that spot is ten games (or twenty points) in the distance. I have written several times that the Leafs MUST put together a multi-game winning streak in order to contend, but they keep falling short. With games tonight in Boston and tomorrow in Buffalo, they have a tough challenge on their hands.

Since the most recent trade with Philly removed a forward without any active player in return, the Leafs have called up Christian Hanson from the Marlies in time for tonight's match in Boston. While action continues day-by-day on the ice, the cellphones are buzzing all around the league as many teams do their best to gear up for this year's stretch run to the post-season.

Hang on to your hats!

Grabovski Brilliant in Leaf Victory

There are lots of good things to report about last night's Leaf win over the Boston Bruins.

Good thing #1 – Phil Kessel finally got the monkey off his back by scoring two goals...his first markers in fifteen games. The Bruin fans booed him every time he got near the puck, but their derision didn't bother him a bit. In addition to snapping his scoring drought, these were the first goals that he has ever scored against his former team since he was traded to Toronto.

Good thing #2 – James Reimer played another strong game in the Toronto net. He continues to provide stalwart work as the Leaf backstop. He plays with increasing confidence, and the rest of the team continues to be confident in his ability to keep them in contention every time out. Reimer's emergence as a big-leaguer is one of the feel-good stories of the Leafs' otherwise frustrating season.

Good thing #3 – Mikhail Grabovski played magnificently last night. He scored two goals... one of them the winner. He literally stuffed this game down the throats of the Bruins after being smashed almost into unconsciousness by Boston's giant, 6-fooy-9 captain, Zdeno Chara. In the final minute of the game, he picked up the puck deep in his own zone, cut to the right, then cut to the left, then squeezed past a Bruin defender and whipped the puck past Tim Thomas in the Boston net. It was a "highlight reel" goal in every sense of the word.

Good thing #4 – The Leafs played like a team last night. They played a full sixty minutes, and they never let up. When they were defending their own turf, they all came back to help. When they were on the attack, they all skated forward into enemy territory. Their passing was MUCH sharper than usual. This was a genuine team victory. Both Joffrey Lupul and Dion Phaneuf contributed two assists each, as well.

NOW COMES BUFFALO...AGAIN! We all know too well how the Leafs normally play in Buffalo. They usually stink out the joint. The last time they played there, I had a feeling that they would play better than usual. I was wrong...DEAD WRONG! They were terrible that night, losing by a 6 – 2 score.

Today, there will be no predictions. I am simply going to kick back, and watch what happens. Will the Leafs be able to carry the momentum that they gathered last night into this game? Or will they skate out onto the ice at HSBC Arena, and fall flat on their faces again? This game promises to be interesting...another huge challenge for a team currently in transition as their General Manager slowly, but surely works to strengthen the lineup trade...after trade...after trade.

Oh, by the way, readers...did you hear about the big secret? Tomas Kaberle is maybe the next Leaf to be traded. How's that for a surprise? Burke says that he can't discuss this topic. He promised to keep everything secret. Kaberle's agent also promised secrecy, so HIS lips are sealed.. Tomas, himself, said after the game last night that it was good to hear that Boston was interested in acquiring his services, but he would rather really stay in Toronto. But, SHHHHHHHHHH… we've got to keep everything secret.

Well Brian, if you are going to keep everything about a potential deal with Boston secret, then please allow me to pick the player on the Boston roster that just might be a suitable choice for the Leafs to get in return for their veteran defenceman.

How about Patrice Bergeron? He has scored 20 goals and has 26 assists. He is a dynamic player. He should be able to play well with Phil Kessel. They'd both have a lot of fun setting each other up for scoring chances.

David Krejci wouldn't be a bad choice either. With 8 goals and 31 assists, he might fit nicely into the Maple Leaf scene.

Brad Marchand would be yet another good possibility. With 15 goals and 16 assists, he looks to me like he is a bona-fide point producer.

<u>Brian…if you can't get at least ONE of these centremen in a deal with Boston…why bother? We have known for months now that the Leafs need help at centre. My three suggestions above are all good choices…GO FOR ONE OF THEM!</u>

Those are my two cents worth.

Joey Crabb Breaks the Jinx

Hallelujah! Praise the Lord! The Leafs have actually won a game in Buffalo!

For the first time in more than two years, the Maple Leafs were able to skate off the ice at the HSBC Arena with two points tucked into their gun-belts. Savour the moment, folks! It may not happen very frequently.

The Leafs are to be commended for this win. They succeeded because they have played the same type of energetic game two nights in a row. First, they beat Boston in their own back yard, and now they accomplished the same result in Western New York. Phil Kessel scored again last night, and now that his goal total has reached 22 on the season, there is no reason to doubt that he will score thirty or more before the regular schedule is put to bed. The winner in this game came off the stick of Joey Crabb. His landmark goal was his very first as a Leaf. It resulted at the end of a very determined effort on his part, fighting off a Sabre defender, and slipping the puck past Ryan Miller in the Buffalo net.

One of the stars of this game was newcomer Joffrey Lupul. He assisted on Kessel's goal last night, and that gives him three points in his first four games. In another word…**production!** I like the looks of this newest Burke acquisition. He may be the answer to a few of the Leafs scoring problems. He appears to have a lot of energy, along with an ability to read the flow of play in the offensive zone. It is going to be interesting to follow his progress over the rest of the schedule.

Phil Kessel is a treat to watch when he is scoring. Man! He is fast on his skates…and if he can get an accurate shot off, it goes into the net like a bullet! I was really getting worried about his state of mind when he was engulfed by his recent scoring slump, but I feel a lot better now that he has broken out of his funk. I wish that I could have a face-to-face talk with him, If I could, here is what I'd say.

"Listen, Phil. You're definitely a point-per-game player. Before each game, sit down on the bench and think about just getting a single point that night. It doesn't matter whether it's a goal or an assist. **Just try for ONE point!** *If that point comes in the first period…mission accomplished! Try for another point as the rest of the game progresses. If you get another, you're obviously having a pretty good game. If time allows, then go for a third."*

My point is this. Phil Kessel is a uniquely talented player. If he can accept in his own mind that this is so, he SHOULD be able to skate out each game comfortable, relaxed, and self-confident in the skills he brings to the game of hockey. He needs to avoid getting too uptight. Goals! ASSISTS! Who cares? A point is a point is a point…and an eighty-two point season is one heckuva success story for ANYONE who suits up in the NHL.

Tomas Kaberle Traded to Boston

Well, dear readers, speculation has become reality. General Manager Brian Burke announced today that Tomas Kaberle has been traded to the Boston Bruins. He has obviously agreed to the trade, waived the no-trade clause in his contract, and will report to his new team in time for this evening's game in Ottawa against the Senators.

In return for Kaberle, the Toronto Maple Leafs will acquire:
- Centre Joe Colborne
- Boston's First Round Draft Pick – 2011 Entry Draft
- Boston's Second Round Conditional Draft Pick – 2012 Entry Draft

Joe Colborne is 21 years of age, and is a native of Calgary, Alberta. He was a first round draft pick of the Bruins in 2008. He played for two years at the University of Denver. Currently, he is tied for the third scoring position on the Bruins' AHL affiliate in Springfield with 12 goals and 14 assists. He will report at once to the Toronto Marlies, where he will play his first game with them tomorrow.

****

It is only appropriate that we pay tribute to Tomas Kaberle as he parts company with the Toronto Maple Leafs. Brian Burke thanked him for his 13-plus years of service to the team. He described Kaberle as a model team member, and thanked him for his contributions to the club, along with his active role in the community.

Toronto has been the only NHL team that Kaberle has played for. He joined the Leafs in 1998. Since then, he has played in 879 games, has scored 83 goals, and added 437 assists, for a total of 520 points. He has represented the Leafs in four NHL All-Star games. He has also periodically worn the "A" on his jersey as a Leaf Assistant Captain.

Tomas has also played for the Czech Republic eight times in Junior World Championships, World Championships, and the Olympics. In 2006, his team won the Olympic Bronze Medal

Speaking personally, I have mixed feelings about Tomas as he departs the team. I view him as a solid performer and team member, but I'd never describe him using the adjective "great". He constantly frustrated me by passing the puck to his team-mates rather than shooting to the net. I rarely considered him as a "tough" defender or particularly eager to sacrifice his body in the shooting lanes. In terms of production, I would venture that he had six good years and six average years.

Tomas Kaberle is most certainly deserving of the appreciation of everyone in the Leaf Nation as he leaves the Maple Leafs. We should all wish him the very best throughout the remainder of his career.

Anderson Stymies Leafs in Senators Debut

The latest skirmish in the so-called "Battle of Ontario" won't go into the record book as much of a spellbinding effort on the part of either side. On an evening when several hundred hometown patrons gave up their seats at the ACC in order to allow a sizable contingent of military personnel to be honoured, the game itself was pretty tame. There wasn't any scoring at all through three complete periods, plus a five minute overtime session.

Kudos, therefore, must be awarded to the two goalies…Jamie Reimer for the Leafs and Craig Anderson, manning the Ottawa net for the very first time in his career. Anderson had just arrived in Ottawa part-way through his new team's game on Friday night…one that they ultimately lost to Tomas Kaberle's new team, the Boston Bruins. Naturally, Anderson wanted to make a good impression with his new buddies, as well as the usual millions of fans watching on "Hockey Night in Canada". He certainly accomplished that objective. The Leafs peppered him with 47 shots in the game, and he stoned them completely.

Reimer was not as busy as his counterpart, but he, too, was successful in holding the Senators at bay with his own shutout effort, stopping 22 shots with impressive efficiency. The deciding shot came in the shootout from the stick of Jason Spezza, who beat the Leaf rookie with a sizzler from a few feet out.

Toronto now has earned 57 points, and are currently tied with my other favourite team, the Florida Panthers, just seven points out of a berth in the post-season. Ottawa has 10 points fewer, and this morning, they sit at the bottom of the Eastern Conference. Although the Leafs (and the Panthers) both hold out some hopes of being in the playoffs, it appears that the Senators have thrown in the towel. This week, they have started the process of literally blowing up the team, sending FOUR players packing. Mike Fisher, Chris Kelly, Jarkko Ruutu, and Brian Elliott are gone GM Bryan Murray has indicated that more changes are being contemplated with the trade deadline now just eight days away.

Murray's Leaf counterpart, Brian Burke has also been jettisoning several players whom he has deemed expendable as the Leafs move forward. First off, Francois Beauchemin was returned to the Anaheim Ducks, from whence he came. Then, Kris Versteeg was dispatched to the Philadelphia Flyers, his third team in the past few months. Finally, just the other day, Burke finally consummated the long-awaited deal with Boston which saw Tomas Kaberle, the longest-serving Leaf on this year's team join the Bruins. As in Ottawa, more personnel changes in Toronto can be expected over the next few days.

Have you noticed how windy the weather has been over the past few days?

Leafs Nip Islanders to Reach Three-Quarter Pole

The Leafs got goals from two of their key players last night, and picked up another valuable brace of points in their quest for the playoffs. First, at 10:13 of the opening period, Clarke MacArthur took a neat pass from line mate Nik Kulemin, and snapped a wrister past Al Montoya in the Islanders net.

In the second period, the visitors tied the game when Matt Moulson got a backhander past Reimer, who was playing with a bad case of indigestion for the first part of the game, and was not feeling well at all. After alerting Ben Scrivens, his backup, Reimer approached the Leaf doctor, who gave him some "magic medicine" for the problem. Reimer was able to stay in the game, and played well enough to be named one of its stars.

The definite highlight of the third period was Phil Kessel's winning goal. He did it all himself, picking up the puck in his own end, skating up the left wing, cutting sharply to the inside, and snapping a blazing shot past Montoya. That was all the scoring needed, as the Leafs played a solid defensive game for the rest of the period.

Last night's victory brings the Leafs to the three-quarter pole. They have played sixty games. They have twenty-two to go. The team has earned fifty-nine points…a winning percentage of 49.1. In other words, they are within a whisker of being able to call themselves a winning team.

A close examination of the League Standings this morning reveals that the Leafs have not made any significant gains since the half-way point in the schedule. The Leafs have flip-flopped positions with the Florida Panthers, but that's about it. Their improved play lately has brought them within six points of the final playoff spot, but Buffalo, Atlanta, and Carolina still must be overcome in order for the Leafs to succeed.

That, my friends, is almost too much to hope for.

While the Leafs are still mathematically in the hunt for the post-season, they are going to have to really put the proverbial pedal to the metal. They are going to need at least 31 out of a possible 44 points…a very tall order indeed. Added to that challenge, we must be ever heedful that the trade deadline is now less than a week away, and Brian Burke has strongly indicated that he is not finished "wheeling and dealing".

The Leafs have won seven of the eleven games that they've played this month. Only three remain. These three upcoming matches will be exceedingly important in determining the team's ultimate destiny. This Leaf team cannot be described as high-scoring group, averaging only 2.5 goals-per-game, but if they can get production from their key players, and combine that with staunch defence, they may just have a chance to realize some success. Let's hope for the best as the season winds down.

The "Head Shot" Crisis in Hockey

From time to time, the Sports News television shows that I watch refer to the fact that Sidney Crosby, arguably the best hockey player on the planet right now, is still not able to suit up for the Pittsburgh Penguins. Sidney has a head injury.

Sidney has a concussion.

Hockey fans everywhere have undoubtedly seen replays of the hit that Sidney took on January 1st near the end of the outdoor match between the Penguins and the Washington Capitals. 68,111 fans in Heinz Stadium also witnessed the hit in person. From the moment of impact, it was clear that Crosby was injured, although the full extent of that injury remained to be determined.

A few days later, Sidney played in a game against the Tampa Bay Lightning in Pittsburgh. He was smashed head-first into the end boards by Victor Hedman. We haven't seen Sidney Crosby on an NHL ice surface since. That game was played on January 5th. That was 8 weeks ago. We now know that Sidney's injuries...the one that started his problem on January 1st, and the one that aggravated it four days later, have caused him to confront an extremely dangerous, **and possibly life-altering situation...**

POST – CONCUSSION SYNDROME.

I just finished reading an article in a recent edition of Maclean's Magazine. It told of the research that is currently being focused on head injuries in sports, and some of the consequences that can follow. It gave several specific examples of players whose careers have been negatively impacted, or even ended by the aftermath of concussions. I was alarmed by the contents of that article.

After I put my magazine down, I came up to my computer, and Googled the latest NHL injury report. It is dated today, and it revealed the following startling information.

As this is written, there are 21 players listed by the NHL as being out of action due to head injuries...19 of them specifically CONCUSSIONS.

My two sources of information today lead me to a couple of conclusions that I would like to place before you:

1. Hockey helmets worn today are reasonably well designed to protect players from a number of types of injury, **but the Maclean's article strongly suggests that they are INADEQUATE to protect the wearer from potential concussions.**
2. The NHL injury statistics reveal that concussions are inordinately responsible for games lost in league play.

It is impossible to predict specifically what the NHL and other hockey organizations are going to do in order to alleviate this very serious crisis in the game. Most hockey fans are aware that the NHL does recognize that the matter of head injuries requires attention. The NHL has imposed more serious disciplinary consequences to players causing major bodily harm to other players. Fines have been increased. Suspensions have been lengthened. Every team has had "in-service" sessions addressing the issue.

Still...<u>MORE NEED TO BE DONE.</u>

There are some things that I would like to see happen in the near future that might be instrumental in reducing the incidence of concussions in the game of hockey. Here are my suggestions:

1. I have always agreed with Don Cherry's suggestion to place little "STOP" signs on the back of hockey uniforms/equipment at every level, but particular in child and youth hockey. They could be sewn onto sweaters in a readily visible location, and placed as stickers on the back of helmets.

2. The "no-touch" rule about icing the puck should be made universal in the game of hockey, both amateur and professional. It already exists in some leagues, both in North America and internationally. This rule would certainly cut down on a great many player collisions in the end zones and corners.

3. Helmet re-design will almost certainly be addressed in the near future, directly as a result of the intense research being carried out by a number of important organizations devoted to reducing injuries to hockey players at every level.

It is my sincere hope that the current crisis of head injuries in the game of hockey can be reduced in the foreseeable future. Hockey has always been a great game, enjoyed by millions. The elimination of life-altering, catastrophic injuries can only make it better.

Kessel Brilliant in Leaf Victory

We all witnessed Phil Kessel at his best last night, when the Maple Leafs handed a stinging defeat to the Montreal Canadiens right in their own arena. The speedy right-winger scored the first two goals for the Leafs in this hard-fought match, and assisted on two others. Tyler Bozak also had a very special night, scoring twice and adding an assist. The other Toronto marker was contributed by defenceman Brett Lebda with his first goal ever as a Maple Leaf.

Two things about this game should be noted. First of all, this was definitely the most important game of the season for the Leafs. The two points claimed by the team elevated the season standing to the 50% level, a position that hasn't been on the record since November 6th. That achievement alone made this game special.

Secondly, the win brought the Leafs to within four points of a playoff spot. The players can now view themselves as realistic challengers for the post-season. Just a couple of weeks ago, there weren't many fans who would venture such an opinion out loud.

The Leafs must now face, head-on, the following harsh reality.

> This team **MUST** earn **a minimum of 30 points** from this point on.
> There are only 42 points available.
> **AN ENORMOUS SURGE IS GOING TO BE REQUIRED.**

The task facing the Maple Leafs is enormous…but **IT IS MATHEMATICALLY POSSIBLE.**

They must face each game one at a time. They must play both offensively and defensively as a team **EVERY TIME OUT**. The goaltending must continue to be above average.

All of a sudden, as the final quarter of the season has arrived, this team faces the situation that can be described as the **IMPROBABLE** becoming **POSSIBLE.**

This is almost too much to hope for…but, as they say…**HOPE SPRINGS ETERNAL!**

Go Leafs…Go!!!!!

Leafs Lose a Stinker, But Pick Up a Single Point

It's a rare night in the NHL when a team scores 5 goals and loses the game, but that's exactly what happened to the Leafs at the Air Canada Centre last night.

This was an exciting game to watch…that's for sure. Eleven goals were scored over the course of the match. The hometown crowd was up and jumping and cheering, particularly in the third period, when it looked like the Leafs might take control of the game. However, that was not destined to happen. Even though the Penguins had played the previous night, and their regular roster was riddled with injuries, they never gave up, and the result was a tie game at the end of regulation time.

Both goalies were off their games in this one. I have always admired the skill and personality of Marc-Andre Fleury ever since he was in Junior hockey, but he was not at his best last night. At the other end of the rink, James Reimer was fighting the puck from start to finish. He looked tired. He needs to sit out a game and gather himself. I hope that Giguere is well enough to start the game in Atlanta this afternoon.

Joffrey Lupul finally scored his first goals as a Leaf, breaking out of his mini-slump with a pair. The other Leaf markers were contributed by Colby Armstrong, Clarke MacArthur, and Dion Phaneuf.

Pittsburgh was rewarded for acquiring Alex Kovalev from Ottawa the other day. The veteran forward celebrated his return to the Penguins by scoring both the first and last goals of this game. Unfortunately, his second marker was the winning goal in the shootout. The other Penguin scorers were Letestu, Jeffrey, Talbot, and Rupp.

Today will be a challenge for the boys in blue and white. They will be resting at their hotel in the sunny south as this is written, but they'll have to be ready for the drop of the puck at 5 o'clock this afternoon. Last night's prolonged game plus an overnight plane ride to Atlanta will test their endurance for certain.

Overshadowing this important game for the Leafs are the three realities that occupy the back of our minds these days:
1. The trade deadline is 27 ½ hours away as this is written,   and
2. Will the Leafs be able to sign Clarke MacArthur to a contract extension?   and
3. Will the Leaf roster undergo any more changes in the next couple of days?

Stay tuned, folks. The next few hours may be either exciting or quiet. Only Brian Burke and his staff have any clue about what might happen…and they aren't telling until events unfold.

Leafs Blow Lead and Lose in Overtime

As I sat and watched the Leaf-Atlanta game on television yesterday afternoon, I felt very uneasy about what was happening before my eyes. The Leafs were having a dreadful time getting their feet going. The Thrashers, on the other hand, were buzzing around the Leaf net like a swarm of hornets.

All of a sudden, things looked like they were changing. First, Nik Kulemin, assisted by his buddies Grabo and MacArthur, got loose on a breakout into Atlanta territory and scored a goal. Then, just a short time later, Phil Kessel swatted a puck out of mid-air, and the Leafs, who were floundering just moments before, were in the lead by a brace of goals.

At that point, I was hoping that the Leafs could continue their offensive push, and add at least one more goal in order to put themselves into a genuine position of strength. However, they just couldn't get things to happen. They just weren't clicking. My sense of unease deepened dramatically in the second period, when a goalmouth collision between Reimer and Evander Kane jolted the young backstop, knocking him face-first to the ice. He got to his feet, and for a couple of minutes it appeared that he was going to be all right. My relief was short-lived. It was obvious that Reimer was NOT all right. His discomfort was somehow relayed to the bench, and J.S. Giguere prepared himself to get into the game.

The game fell apart for Toronto in the third period. In his post-game remarks, Coach Ron Wilson attributed his team's inability to perform to the fact that "there was nothing left in the tank". The Leafs were too tired to hang on to their lead. The Thrashers, who needed points just as badly as did the Leafs, chipped away with goals by Ladd and Stapleton, and the game ended in a 2 – 2 tie. A final goal by Hainsey at the 2:31 mark of the overtime session assured the home team of the extra point.

I attribute the inability of the Leafs to keep up their energy level to a quirk of scheduling on the part of the NHL. As a former educator, with plenty of experience in the art of setting up timetables, I know how challenging it can be. I am also aware that the NHL must arrange a schedule for a total of 1230 games...a humungous challenge to be sure. Still, I believe that there should be a MINIMUM of 24 hours between games for any given team. The Leafs played a game on Saturday evening that went all the way to a shootout. Then, they had to get to the airport, board their plane, fly to Atlanta, transfer to their hotel, get some sleep, wake up and go through the obligatory cycle of activities to prepare for a 5:00 P.M. puck drop against the Thrashers. That's asking a lot when one considers the physical toll exacted by play in the National Hockey League.

Oh well, at least the Leafs got a point from this one. We should be thankful, I guess. The team now has a few days to recover before facing Pittsburgh at home on Wednesday night.

Summary of Maple Leaf Trade Activity

With the trade deadline having expired yesterday at 3:00 P.M., we can now sit back and examine exactly the situation that the franchise now confronts as the 2010 – 2011 season enters its final quarter. The roster is now set for the stretch run, and to the great surprise of most Leaf fans, it appears that the Leafs are going to be a part of that run.

Today, I will summarize all of the trade activity conducted and concluded by Brian Burke and his management team. I want to be clear that all of the deals consummated have not been the labour of just one man, Brian Burke, even though the media will praise him almost exclusively if the moves turn out well. If they don't pan out, they will inevitably heap blame, scorn, and derision mercilessly upon him. The reality is that all of the decisions outlined below have resulted from hours of meetings, consultations, phone calls, e-mails, and sleepless nights shared by many management and scouting employees of the hockey club.

Over the past few weeks, the transactions concluded are:

Leaving Toronto	To
Francois Beauchemin	Anaheim Ducks
Kris Versteeg	Philadelphia Flyers
Tomas Kaberle	Boston Bruins
John Mitchell	New York Rangers
Conditional 7th Round Draft Pick – 2011	Anaheim

Coming to Torontov	From
Joffrey Lupul – Forward (Leafs)	Anaheim
Jake Gardiner – Defence (Prospect)	Anaheim
Conditional 4th Round Draft Pick – 2013	Anaheim
1st Round Draft Pick – 2011	Philadelphia
3rd Round Draft Pick – 2011	Philadelphia
Joe Colborne – Forward (Marlies)	Boston
1st Round Draft Pick – 2011	Boston
2nd Round Draft Pick – 2012	Boston
7th Round Draft Pick – 2012	New York
Aaron Voros (Marlies)	Anaheim

Only time will tell how these deals will play out. My cursory examination leads me to think positively about them. I like the way that Joffrey Lupul appears to be gaining some momentum as a Leaf. Joe Colborne and Aaron Voros are already impacting on the score sheets with their new Marlie team-mates. I love the fact that the Leafs are going to have three fairly early draft picks in June of this year. Jake Gardiner has been touted as a very promising prospect. All in all, the Leaf future looks a little brighter this morning.

Phil Kessel Named as NHL Player of the Week

Congratulations are certainly due to Phil Kessel, announced as the Number One player of the week ending February 27th. There is no doubt that he has played a major role in the recent surge experienced by the Leafs that has propelled them almost unexpectedly into the race for a playoff position. Every aspect of his game has picked up lately. A very good skater, he has used his speed to get himself into scoring position…sometimes overpowering defenders as he breaks toward the net. His defensive game has also improved. He is making more of an effort to persevere in his team's defensive zone, attempting to disrupt the opposition attacks, seize the puck, and head full bore onto the attack.

Almost all season long, there has been a lot of talk and conjecture about acquiring a centreman who could combine effectively with Kessel to pose a consistent scoring threat on the Leaf attack. Thus far, all efforts have fallen short. It almost appears that Kessel himself has decided to wait no longer, and make himself into a legitimate threat with or without much help from anyone. I hope that his inspired type of play continues, because if the Leafs ARE destined to make the playoffs, the team is going to need Kessel AND the other scoring leaders on the team to play their best…every game out.

Phil Kessel is THE individual designated by Brian Burke to be the "franchise" player for the Leafs. One of the first things that Burke did after he had been named the Maple Leaf General Manager was to acquire Kessel from the Boston Bruins. In order to do so, Burke had to relinquish first and second round draft picks… a very steep price to pay.

Why was Brian Burke so eager to acquire this particular player and make him the cornerstone of the team? Let's take a look at this young man's career to see if we can understand Burke's rationale.

Burke is an American. It is only natural that, in his line of work, Brian is constantly keeping himself attuned to hockey prospects coming out of the USA. Burke himself is a product of the American hockey system. He is highly regarded by the "powers that be" in the USA. It can be strongly argued that Burke's reputation as an expert in hockey is world-wide.

Kessel is an American, too. Philip Joseph Kessel Jr. was born on October 2, 1987 in Madison, Wisconsin He is 23 years of age. A kid's hockey career usually begins to take off when he plays Bantam and Midget hockey. When Phil played Bantam in 2001 – 2002, at the age of 14, he scored 286 points in 86 games. (3.3 points per game)

The next year, playing Midget at age 15, he scored 158 points in 71 games. (2.2 points per game)

For the next two years, Phil took part in the National Development Program, and participated in both National and International tournaments. In regular season play, he scored 180 points in 109 games. (1.6 points per game)

In his final year as a Junior (age 18), Phil was still scoring at a rate in excess of a point per game, and that, I have always believed, elevates him to the rank of **superstar.**

In the 2006 NHL Entry Draft, Phil was considered to be the fourth-best North American hockey player, and was picked fifth by the Boston Bruins.

Early in the December of 2006, before he was even twenty years old, Phil learned that he had become the victim of a serious illness. Specifically, he had contracted testicular cancer. At this point, readers, I suggest that we take a moment to contemplate just how great an impact such a diagnosis probably had on a kid as young as Phil. Many of us, myself included, have been directly affected by cancer. In 2003, my wife, Charlotte, became very ill with a form of cancer. She very nearly died, and spent about a month recovering in Henderson Hospital in Hamilton. She experienced another serious illness shortly after that, and for the next five years we both had some very anxious times. Every blood test and every doctor's appointment brought anxiety that only diminished when we got favourable reports from one doctor after another. Dealing with cancer is life-altering at any age, and many young people are ill-equipped to deal with it.

Kessel underwent cancer surgery, and returned to action with the Bruins after missing only eleven games. In June of 2007, Phil was awarded the Bill Masterton Award, recognizing his dedication to hockey in the face of adversity. Being awarded the Masterton Trophy at such a young age speaks volumes about his eagerness to become successful as a professional athlete.

In three regular seasons with the Boston Bruins, Phil scored 66 goals and 60 assists for a total of 126 points in 222 games. The Bruins made the playoffs following each of his final two seasons with them, and Phil recorded 15 points in those games.

Late in the 2009 season, Phil sustained a shoulder injury that turned out to require surgery during the off-season. Then, in September of that year, he was traded to Toronto. Last year, his first as a Leaf, he scored 30 goals and added 25 assists in the 55 games that he was able to play following his late season start due to the surgery.

The current season has not been very kind to either Phil or the Leafs. He went through an extended and well documented scoring drought, from which he has recently emerged. As this is written, it appears that he will reach or exceed the thirty-goal mark, and we all hope that his energy and skill will help lead the Leafs to the post-season. It is clear that Phil Kessel is still a remarkably talented athlete, well worth the confidence that Brian Burke has always placed in him. There is every reason to believe that, over time, Kessel has the ability to forge an outstanding career as this young Maple Leaf team builds towards a future Stanley Cup Championship.

Another Win…Let the Good Times Roll!

Yahoo! Fun is starting to return to Maple Leaf hockey!

Last night, a full house at the ACC went home deliriously happy after watching the Leafs eke out a 3 – 2 overtime win against the Penguins. This win came courtesy of three of the team's top players. Kulemin, Kessel, and Grabovski each contributed a goal and another couple of points was added to the club's record.

Now that the roster of the Leafs has been set for the remainder of the season, I believe that the players have realized, almost too late, that the ultimate destiny of this year's club is going to be decided on the ice. Management can do no more. The trade deadline has come and gone. The coaching staff, by this point in the season, will probably have very few new wrinkles to impart to the players. Execution! That will be the key word that needs to be fulfilled night in and night out if the promised land of the post-season is to be reached.

Who are the players most responsible for getting this team to within four points of their objective…stated so many months ago by their erstwhile General Manager? Who are the players who will need to come up with their very best efforts if the Leafs are to be successful?

In order to answer my first question, I will report to you the revelations of just one of the several charts that I maintain on a daily basis to help me with my writing. I have kept track of the so-called "three stars" of each game, all season long. According to my calculations, the players who have carried the Leafs to their current, lofty, tenth place in the Eastern Conference are:

Mikhail Grabovski	15 Stars
Phil Kessel	14 Stars
James Reimer	8 Stars

Honourable mentions should go to Tyler Bozak (6),   Clarke MacArthur (5), Luke Schenn (5), Nik Kulemin (5), and Tomas Kaberle (5).

With Kaberle recently dispatched to the Boston Bruins, there clearly needs to be some "stepping up" by several others on the roster. I would urge the following to accelerate their work, and join the banner group listed above:

J. S. Giguere	4 Stars	
Colby Armstrong	4 Stars	
Joffrey Lupul	2 Stars	(Newcomer)
Dion Phaneuf	*1 Star*	

Phaneuf is one player who REALLY needs to inject himself forcefully into the picture portrayed here. **<u>Captain Dion Phaneuf has been chosen as a star in only ONE SINGLE GAME THIS SEASON.</u>** His play has improved to some extent lately, but all in all, his record as the team's leader on the ice is lamentable.

You may have noticed that I have not included another player in my list to those needing to "step forward and be counted." Jonas Gustavsson has been announced as one of the game's three stars on FOUR occasions this season. Back in October, I think that most of us in Leaf Nation expected to see him claim a role as the Leafs' goaltender of the future. Sadly, that has not happened. For the most part, his performances in the net have been disappointing. It appeared that he lost the confidence of his team-mates. His play would suggest that his own self-confidence took a hit, although he would probably deny that. To further complicate his situation, his heart condition cropped up again, for the third time in less than two years. I am really beginning to question whether or not Jonas's future in the Maple Leaf organization is as bright as it once was.

At this writing, it seems that James Reimer has laid claim to the role as the heir apparent to the Maple Leafs' prime goaltending role.

At any rate, I have listed ELEVEN players above who, in my opinion, must STAND and DELIVER over the course of the next 18 games. The other members of the supporting cast each have responsibilities to carry out in order to augment the efforts of the lead actors.

Tonight will see the challenge intensify, as the Leafs take to the ice in Philadelphia. Right now, the Flyers stand FIRST in the Eastern Conference, and SECOND in the league. Contrary to its designation as "The City of Brotherly Love", I don't expect a whole lot of love to be dispensed by either team this evening. I rather believe that we may be confronted by a twenty-first century version of "the Broad Street Bullies".

I will report, tomorrow, concerning which team prevails in this classic event.

Leafs Stun Flyers in Philly

Don't pinch me! I'm having a wonderful dream, and I don't want to waken up!

As I sat in my living room watching the Leafs and the Flyers struggle for superiority in a 2 – 2 tie in the third period last night, I decided that I'd be happy if the boys in the white uniforms could come away with a single point. To that juncture in the match, it looked like the hockey gods were conspiring once again against the Leafs. Toronto had matched the Flyers goal for goal through the first two frames of the game, thanks to Nik Kulemin and Dion Phaneuf.

But guess who had scored BOTH of the Philly goals?

It was none other than Kris Versteeg! Yes! The same Kris Versteeg who had spent the first five months of the season patrolling right wing for the Leafs. It was starting to look like he might just score one more, and exact a measure of revenge upon Burkie's boys for dumping him to one of the top teams in the league. (If you can call that "dumping")

Then, suddenly, Darryl Boyce picked up the puck deep in the Flyer defensive zone, fought his way to the blue paint, and sneaked the puck past the goalie and a Philadelphia defender into the net. I could hardly believe my eyes!

All the Leafs had to do for the rest of the period was hold on and defend their lead.. They often have trouble doing that, though, and last night was no exception. Rookie Keith Aulie attempted to clear the puck out of the Toronto zone in the dying moments of the game, but failed. The ensuing uproar in front of the Leaf net almost ruined the evening, but James Reimer came through again, literally snatching victory from the jaws of defeat with his trusty catching glove.

Boyce was the only Leaf named as a star in this game, but full marks must also be awarded to both Kulemin and Phaneuf, each of whom picked up two points for their work. As always, Jamie Reimer's solid performance in the Toronto net was invaluable, and the steady performances across the roster assured ultimate success.

I hope that my happy slumber, complete with its vision of sugarplums can continue on Saturday, when the Cup-winning Chicago Blackhawks visit the ACC. I don't want this bubble to burst! Watching hockey on my HD television set has suddenly become fun! The Leafs are starting to look like a bunch of pretty happy guys. Wouldn't it be nice if they can keep this big, shiny bubble intact until at least mid-April?

Then, we could all enjoy the silver lining of a very happy summer!

Setback #1 - Leafs Smacked Early by Cup Champs

This coming Friday, President Obama will be entertaining a very impressive contingent of guests from his home jurisdiction. As has been the custom over the past few years, the Stanley Cup champions will be visiting the White House in order to receive the accolades of the Leader of the Free World. This time, the Chicago Blackhawks will afford the President an opportunity to see the Cup up close and personal. The Hawks also will probably present Mr. Obama with a championship jersey emblazoned with his name.

Last night, the Blackhawks visited the Air Canada Centre. There was little in the way of ceremony involved. As things turned out, there was nothing to celebrate. The Hawks opened the game with their impressive speed and shooting accuracy, In a first period that was totally dominated by the visitors from the Windy City, goals by Hossa, Frolik, and Toews put the Leafs in a very deep hole. The goals resulted from costly Leaf mistakes.

Although Joffrey Lupul snapped one past Crawford in the Blackhawk net early in the second period, two more goals by Stalberg and Bickell pretty well salted the game away for Chicago.

The Leafs made a valiant attempt in the third to get back into the game. Joey Crabb scored his second goal of the season early in the period. Then, with less than a minute left in the game, Luke Schenn drilled home his third. Unfortunately, that was all the home team could muster.

This loss did not surprise anyone either attending the game or watching on television. The Hawks skated onto the ice looking for their eighth consecutive win, and they eventually got it. From all appearances they are rounding out the season very prepared to defend their title. The Hawks are a fast-skating club, blessed with several very impressive scorers as well as solid defenders. Crawford and Turco both offer the champions some staunch goalkeeping skills.

Although there were no Leafs among the three stars of the game, they did indeed pick up their performance in the second half of the match. I hope that Lupul's goal was a sign that he is finding his scoring range. He is definitely going to be needed down the stretch. Luke Schenn continues to impress me with his improved defensive skills and strong physical play.

The Leafs will face three opponents in the coming week. On Tuesday, they will travel to the Big Apple to have a set-to with the Islanders. Thursday and Saturday will feature key matches with Philadelphia and Buffalo. We may have a clearer picture one week from now about whether or not the playoffs are a genuine possibility, or an illusion.

Leafs Gain Ground In Spite of OT Loss

I find it very difficult to understand why it is so complicated to motivate professional athletes when a given situation is so obviously critical. Every single player on the Maple Leafs knows how important it is to win every point that they can. Yet, they came out of the gate last night against an Islander team that will NOT make the playoffs this year and stood around watching as the home club dominated during the early stages of the match. The Leafs were lucky to escape the first period with the score tied at 0 – 0.

Once again, for the umpteenth time this season, the Leafs fell behind in the second period following a tip-in goal by Islander Zenon Konopka. Just a few seconds later, though, Keith Aulie snapped in his very first NHL goal, assisted by Tim Brent and Jay Rosehill. Frans Nielsen put the home team ahead for the second time in the game, but Tim Brent, playing one of his best games as a Leaf, tied the score before the middle frame had ended.

The teams traded goals near the mid-point of the third period. First, Grabner put the home team ahead, but the lead was short-lived when Kulemin tied the score for the Leafs. I felt a degree of relief at the end of regulation time, knowing that the boys in blue and white had secured one point, and had a chance for another in overtime. However, at 4:02 of the extra period, Blake Comeau tipped in a blast from the point past Reimer, and Toronto relinquished the extra point. In spite of that, they were able to get a point closer to a playoff position because the Buffalo Sabres lost their game to Carolina.

It was clear from both the content and the tone of Ron Wilson's remarks to the media following the game that he was not pleased that all hands had not reported on deck for this important match-up. He had praise for his third-liners, who were responsible for two of the three Leaf markers, but clearly projected his disappointment in the efforts of some of his so-called "front-liners".

Beginning tomorrow night, the Leafs will be engrossed in a critical home stand at the ACC that could determine their ultimate destiny this season. On Thursday, Saturday, and Monday, they will host, in order, the Philadelphia Flyers, the Buffalo Sabres, and the Tampa Bay Lightning. A total of more than sixty thousand roaring fans…and millions more watching on television will be **EXPECTING** nothing but a supreme effort **EVERY TIME OUT!** Talk about accountability… the Leafs are staring it in the face in these three games. By ten o'clock next Monday evening, they could be still in the thick of a playoff stretch run, or wallowing in the dust as also-rans.

Heroes or Bums…every member of the Maple Leafs confronts not one, but THREE judgment days.

WHO will be WHAT? HOW MANY of WHICH will prevail? The count starts on Thursday.

Leafs Try Hard, But Lose a Critical Game

Please note the date above. As this is written, the nation of Japan is coping with a 9.8 earthquake and its after-effects. There has been horrendous loss of life and property. It has been a catastrophe of historic proportion.

In the face of such a disaster, a hockey game means little, or nothing. The report that follows is a bare-bones assessment of this game.

In spite of a strong effort, the Maple Leafs lost to a better team last night.

They were hampered by the ejection of Mike Komisarek early in the match for cross-checking Philly Daniel Carcillo into the boards, forcing Ron Wilson to utilize only five defencemen.

Philadelphia scorers were Meszaros, Powe, and Giroux.

Joffrey Lupul and Mikhail Grabovski replied for the Leafs.

Toronto is now positioned SIX POINTS out of the final playoff position.

Their next match, Saturday against Buffalo, will be the most critical game of the season to date. A loss will be devastating to Leaf chances of making the post season.

March 12, 2011

Some Random Thoughts

Tonight's Game

For tonight's game at the ACC between the Leafs and the Sabres, every hockey cliché in the book will apply.

This game will separate the men from the boys…the sheep from the goats…the wheat from the chaff…and on…and on…and on!

Buffalo has 74 points…and stands 7th in the Eastern Conference.
Toronto has 68 points…and stands 10th.
A Leaf win will give them 70 points…just 4 behind the Sabres.
A Leaf loss will give the Sabres 76 points…8 points more than Toronto
This is a four-point game!

Every Leaf player MUST realize that the game starts at 00:00 on the time clock, and ends at 60:00. **The Leaf season is ON THE LINE tonight.**

Go, Leafs…GO!

THE "HEAD-SHOT ISSUE"

On Tuesday night, just three days ago, Zdeno Chara of the Boston Bruins checked Max Pacioretty of the Montreal Canadiens head-first into the turnbuckle between the benches at the Bell Centre. Pacioretty sustained a broken vertebrae AND a concussion. The replay of this incident has been played virtually HUNDREDS of times on every television channel in the Western World.

It was a vicious check. Chara received a 5 minute major penalty, and a game misconduct. THAT'S ALL!

Just a couple of weeks ago, I wrote in this work that there were 22 players on the NHL Injured List due to concussion injuries. Yesterday, I heard a media report that there have, in actual fact, been 72 concussion injuries so far this season.

THAT FIGURE REPRESENTS ALMOST 10 PERCENT OF THE PLAYERS IN THE NHL!

126

Since the Chara-Pacioretty incident, there have been MANY concerns expressed about the NHL's lack of appropriate disciplinary response.

The Prime Minister of Canada has expressed his concern.
The Premier of Quebec added his voice to the chorus of dismay.
Air Canada has written to the NHL, threatening to withdraw sponsorship money.
VIA Rail has also written to the league, expressing great concern.

What has been Commissioner Gary Bettman's response to all this?

He defended the decision of the NHL's Disciplinary Personnel who decided that no further action was required following the Chara check, and told Air Canada that if they wanted to withdraw their money, the NHL would find another airline to replace them.

Gary…wake up and smell the coffee! <u>YOU (the NHL) HAVE A CRISIS ON YOUR HANDS!</u>

Head injuries among the players have reached **<u>UNACCEPTABLE</u>** levels.

Players are not respecting other players.

Hockey has become very fast and more dangerous due to modern technology in the realm of skates and protective equipment.

Currently, the helmets worn by NHL players are proving to be **<u>ABSOLUTELY USELESS</u>** when it comes to preventing concussions.

Next week, in Florida, the General Managers will meet, and the head injury issue will be front and centre.

<u>IT IS TIME FOR THE NHL TO ACT.</u>

<u>THIS CRISIS IS NOT GOING AWAY UNTIL THE LEAGUE AND THE PLAYERS DO SOMETHING TO ADDRESS THIS SERIOUS SITUATION.</u>

<u>PLEASE ACT……BEFORE A PLAYER DIES ON THE ICE.</u>

Leafs Prevail: Hopes for Playoffs Live On

Early yesterday, a television reporter asked Ron Wilson if he felt that his players were nervous approaching last night's crucial game at the ACC. His reply hit the nail on the head.

"Nervous!" He replied. "Why would anybody who ever played hockey in a driveway while growing up be nervous? These are the kinds of games that you dream about playing in some day!"

Wilson was absolutely right, and last night we saw two teams that both wanted to win very badly. Only one could come out on top, and, to the great delight of everyone in Leaf Nation, it was the Maple Leafs who triumphed.

The teams traded goals in the first period…Weber scoring for the Sabres, and Clarke MacArthur notching his 20th to tie the score.

In the second frame, Bozak, assisted by Kessel and Lupul, scored his 11th of the season. Unfortunately, Buffalo stepped up their effort and took the lead, thanks to goals by Hecht and Leopold. The players skated off the ice at the second intermission with the visitors in the lead.

The Leafs then faced what has been the most important twenty minutes of their season to date. They had to win. There was no other option. **AND WIN THEY DID!** Thanks to goals by two of the team's star players, Mikhail Grabovski and Phil Kessel, the Leafs pulled ahead, and forcefully defended their lead until the final buzzer sounded. I was impressed to see the Leafs saluting their fans by raising their sticks skyward as they skated to their dressing room. The fans were roaring their support all through the game, and their raucous participation was instrumental in gaining last night's brace of points.

So, readers, the Maple Leaf surge continues. After having a day to savour their success, they will suit up again on Monday when the Tampa Bay Lightning come to town. There can be no let up. Every game is important. Last night's win was a genuine morale booster. Let's hope that they can keep moving ahead, because there are several very good teams that they still have to pass in order to achieve the season's central objective…the post-season!

Waiting for the Math

There is a lot of doom and gloom throughout the sports media this morning. Whether you look at the newspaper, listen to the radio, or watch television, everyone is writing off the Leaf playoff hopes. All this following last night's match at the ACC, when the Leafs came out as flat as p*** on a platter, and got smeared by the Tampa Bay Lightning to the tune of 6 to 2.

I'm not going to join the chorus. I'm too stubborn to throw in the towel. I prefer to wait until the Leafs are mathematically eliminated from any possibility of the playoffs. There are still 12 games left to be played. That adds up to 24 points. Faint hope still exists.

None of the Maple Leafs were named as a star in this game. Everyone was off his game. Reimer was fighting the puck from the get-go. The Lightning had his number, stinging him for five goals before Ron Wilson decided that enough was enough, and took him out of the net just before the midway point of the third period. J. S. Giguere gave up the sixth, and final Tampa Bay goal.

Let's face it, readers, the Lightning is a far better team than the Leafs. They have 87 points, while the Leafs have just 70. Why all the moaning and groaning? It would have been an upset of huge proportion if the Leafs had won.

The Lightning scorers last night were Thompson, Ritola (2), Lecavalier, Moore, and Lundin. Phaneuf got his 5th for the Leafs, and Kulemin his 26th.

Just to make matters worse, we learned following the game that Colby Armstrong sustained a broken foot when he blocked a shot in the second period. That probably means that he is done for the season. That signifies a profound loss of energy for the Leafs as they enter the home stretch. They will have to dig a lot deeper to compensate for his absence from the lineup.

The boys now hit the road for their next two games…Carolina on Wednesday night, and the Florida Panthers on Thursday. Nobody will need to remind them about the importance of these two matches. If they lose them, the Math that I am waiting for gets scary…REAL SCARY!

Phaneuf and Reimer Inspire Leafs to Victory

I am sure that everyone in Leaf Nation can appreciate my reasons for not giving up my hopes for a Leaf role in this year's post-season. Last night's win over the Carolina Hurricane made me proud to be a Leaf fan. The boys won the game with a sudden outburst of scoring in the middle of the second period, and followed up with a staunch and unyielding defence of their lead. Another must-win effort on enemy ice! Wow!

There were two stars of last night's game whose efforts merit special mention. First of all, team captain Dion Phaneuf played a remarkable game, scoring two goals, and assisting on the winner by Darryl Boyce. He was a tower of power and leadership to his young colleagues in this game.

Dion has taken a lot of heat lately. The media has been very critical of him, sometimes suggesting that he has lurked under the respective shadows of Francois Beauchemin and Tomas Kaberle for the greater part of the season. With both of those players now playing for Anaheim and Boston respectively, sports reporters have claimed that Phaneuf has finally seized his role as captain, and is now emerging to assert his legitimacy as team leader.

I don't buy that opinion without reservation. While there may be some truth to that argument, I believe that Dion's injury has had more to do with his modest success on the ice this year than we may ever understand. It was in the first game in November that he sustained a SEVERE cut on the back of his left leg while playing the Ottawa Senators. That cut was so deep that it had to be surgically repaired, and required WEEKS of recovery time. Only Phaneuf himself knows the pain that he went through. Only he really knows the true toll exacted throughout those few tough weeks out of the lineup. Once he was able to play again, it undoubtedly took several games before he could really perform to a 100% level.

What can one say about James Reimer. He had a lousy game on Monday night. The whole team stunk out the joint. Then, he had his 23rd birthday on Tuesday. It must have been at least a little bit happy, because he came out again last night and made some brilliant saves against a very feisty Carolina hockey club. This kid has turned out to be one of the most positive elements of this year's Leaf story. His role in the team's revival has been MONUMENTAL.

The Leafs have another critical game tonight in Sunrise Florida against the Panthers. They cannot afford to let up. They MUST win. I am extremely sorry about what has happened to the Panthers lately. They are my second-favourite team in the NHL due to my acquaintance with Shawn Matthias, who plays for them, and my friendship with Shawn's grandfather. However, my primary loyalty lies with the Leafs.
    Go, Leafs.....Go!

Leafs Run Out of Gas in Florida

This particular game meant absolutely nothing to the Florida Panthers. We all know how much it COULD have meant to the Leafs. As things turned out, it was pretty much a wipeout for both teams.

This was a dull, uninteresting game to watch.

The Leafs brought NOTHING to the rink.

Giguere was not sharp, letting in three of the four Florida markers. The final Panther goal was scored into an empty net when Wilson lifted Giguere for an extra attacker during a third-period power (?) play.

Jamie Reimer didn't even dress for this game. Gustavsson was the designated backup for the night. Jamie deserved the rest.

The four Panther goals were scored by Samsonov, Weiss. Santorelli, and Ellerby.

The Leafs sure picked a bad time to come up with such a bummer of a game.

I hope that they can do a lot better on Saturday.

<u>Celebrating the Leaf Lesser-Lights</u>

As I watched last night's Leaf/Bruin hockey game on television, and the game unfolded to my great delight, much was being made by the commentators about the frustrations evident among the Bruin team. Claude Julien, Boston's head coach, was clearly not pleased with the efforts of his players. The players were frustrated, shaking their heads at several blown plays, and looking skyward as if wondering what the hockey gods were up to. Tukka Rask went in to replace a shaky Tim Thomas. When the Leafs scored on him, he yelled at his defence colleagues, and soon found himself back on the bench as punishment. The language heard the length of the Bruin bench was unprintable.

What was going on? It seemed clear that the Boston game plan was in a shambles.

Perhaps their plan was to keep the big Leaf scorers off the scoreboard. Perhaps shadows were assigned to guys like Kessel, Grabovski, Kulemin, MacArthur, et al. Perhaps they forgot all about their supporting cast…guys named Kadri, Crabb, Aulie, Brown, and Schenn. With the exception of Luke Schenn, last night's scorers could certainly be regarded as "lesser-lights".

Nazem Kadri just got called up from the Marlies this past week. His first period marker was the very first goal of his NHL career. He later added an assist. Joey Crabb had a career night, with two goals and an assist. Keith Aulie got the second goal of his career, and finally Mike Brown, a tenacious hard worker, scored his third goal of the season. And, of course, this entire mini-outburst of power was backstopped by another splendid piece of work by Jamie Reimer, back in the Leaf net following his day off in Florida.

Their win against the Beantowners last night keeps the Leafs in the playoff race. You may recall that back on February 24th, it was generally decided that the Leafs had to begin a plan of attack…a sort of SURGE if they really wanted to win a playoff position. As of this morning, they have achieved 15 of the 30 points that are going to be needed in order to even get close. Even if they succeed, 30 points may still not be enough. They MUST get fifteen more points in the next 9 games…an almost impossible task.

Who was it that once said, "HOPE IS WHERE THE HEART IS"?

Everyone in Leaf Nation knows where our hearts are. There is still hope.

Go Leafs…GO!

There are three games during the coming week, against Minnesota, Colorado, and Detroit. Every one of those games are critical…in the extreme!

The NHL Stretch Run Examined

It is now quite late in the NHL season. By and large, it is accurate to say that all teams have at least nine, but no more than eleven games remaining to be played. My purpose today will be to summarize for all my readers what has happened to this point in the schedule, and what remains in the days ahead leading up to the final games to be played on April 10th. My remarks will cover both the Eastern and Western Conferences of the National Hockey League.

I have spent the better part of the last two days closely examining the "lay of the land" in both conferences. As this drive to the finish stands, of the thirty teams in the League, I see ELEVEN teams engaged in keen competition for playoff positions…six in the Western Conference, and five in the East.

If there is a "magic number" of points required for a team to make the playoffs, it could be argued that 90 would be that level of achievement. That figure is not hard and fast, or etched in stone, but any team achieving fewer than 90 points should be considered a long shot for the post-season. Keeping that in mind, I offer the following interpretation of the standings as of today's date.

Looking first at the western clubs, it is my feeling that the Edmonton Oilers and Colorado Avalanche will fail to make the playoffs this year. Neither club currently has enough points to even get to the 90 mark. At the other end of the scale, the Vancouver Canucks have literally run away with the conference. They currently possess 103 points, and have nine games remaining. The Canucks are currently the best team in the NHL. Of course, they will make the post-season, and joining them, based upon where things stand right now should be the following clubs:

Detroit Red Wings	San Jose Sharks
Phoenix Coyotes	Los Angeles Kings
Chicago Blackhawks	Nashville Predators

This situation means that there are literally six clubs competing for the single remaining playoff position, and those organizations follow:

Anaheim Ducks	Dallas Stars
Calgary Flames	Minnesota Wild
Columbus Blue Jackets	St. Louis Blues

In the Eastern Conference, an equally exciting race has emerged. There, three organizations will finish the regular season on the outside, looking in. The Ottawa Senators, New York Islanders, and Florida Panthers find themselves at the low end of the totem pole. There have been two clubs leading the pack in the East, those being the Philadelphia Flyers and the Washington Capitals. In my view, they will be competing in the playoffs against the following teams:

Boston Bruins	Pittsburgh Penguins
Tampa Bay Lightning	Montreal Canadiens
New York Rangers	

Just as is the case in the West, that leaves a single spot left to be decided. Competing for that spot will be these clubs:

Buffalo Sabres	Carolina Hurricane
Toronto Maple Leafs	New Jersey Devils
Atlanta Thrashers	

The next three weeks should be very exciting for hockey fans who follow the NHL. One third of the league will be fighting for their playoff lives. The five teams that, for all intents and purposes will NOT be playoff bound will relish their roles as "spoilers" to the eleven clubs that will be trying to claw their way into the couple of vacancies still up for grabs.

The scene, therefore, is set. The stakes are high. In addition to the prestige of appearing in the NHL's "second season", the successful organizations stand to make millions of dollars in additional revenue, some to the tune of close to a million dollars per game. It will be just as the old saying goes…"to the victors belong the spoils".

And…at the end of the season, just as summer glows closely ahead, there is The Cup… that gleaming, silver trophy that every hockey player alive wants to lift to the heavens…LORD STANLEY'S CHALICE!

This stretch run should be a blast!

Enjoy!

Leafs Keep Pace with Win over Wild

It was a very special night at the Excel Energy Center in St. Paul last evening, when the Toronto Maple Leafs paid a rare visit to the place called home by the Minnesota Wild. A whole bunch of Canadians had made a long, 700 km. drive from the Arborg area of Manitoba to watch a native son play hockey. They would not be cheering for the home team…or anyone on it. The object of their interest and affection this night would be James Reimer, the young goalie for the visiting Toronto Maple Leafs.

He would not disappoint this contingent from his home town. Among the group were his mom and dad, along with several other friends and family members. James had made certain that they were seated amidst the sellout crowd for this match. Jamie and his Maple Leaf pals played a very disciplined defensive game, and defeated the home team in their own rink.

To put the icing on this cake, Jamie posted a shutout. How's THAT for a fairy-tale ending to this story?

The Leafs did what they had to do last night. They scored a goal in each of the three periods, and kept the home team off the scoreboard completely. In the first stanza, it was Joffrey Lupul scoring his tenth goal of the season. Mikhail Grabovski made it 2 – 0 in the second with his 28th, and Carl Gunnarsson pumped in his 5th, an insurance marker in the third. Reimer played another solid game in the net, and posted his sixteenth win of the season. This young man, who just turned 23 a few days ago, has become a bona-fide superstar for the Maple Leafs since his arrival on the scene.

I wish that I could tell you that the Leafs gained some ground in the race for a playoff position, but I can't. All of the other teams in contention won their games, too. So, the Leafs are still in the hunt, but they are now down to eight matches remaining to be played. On Thursday, the Leafs will face another tough opponent in the Colorado Avalanche…another must-win situation.

As I watched the game on television last night, and took in the effort and energy of this young Leaf squad, I could not help but feel good about their future prospects. They were having fun out there. There were no slackers. Everyone was intent on putting forth a good effort…and their work paid off. Right now, we're watching a bunch of kids having fun playing a game that they love, and even if it may turn out to be too little, too late, they've certainly made the last part of the season a lot of fun to watch.

Keep up the good work, boys!

Doing What They Gotta Do

When speaking about some of the necessary tasks in life that we all face and are obliged to overcome, we are sometimes inclined to shrug our shoulders and say, "Ya gotta do what ya gotta do."

Right now, that is precisely what the Toronto Maple Leafs are doing. They've gotta win… plain and simple! And, to their credit, they ARE winning! They are being inspired by a young (23) farm boy from Manitoba with an engaging, sheepish grin, who joined this hockey club midway through the season, and has become a bona-fide star. James Reimer is having the time of his life. At this writing, he is the winningest goalie of the three who have guarded the Leaf net this season. Last night's victory was his 17th.

On December 20th, 2010 Reimer skated out late in the third period of a game between the Leafs and the Atlanta Thrashers to replace Giguere, who had sustained an injury. He faced a total of 4 shots, and stopped them all. Slowly, but surely…day by day…game after game, Jamie has elevated himself to his present position as THE number one goalie for this team of youngsters. Due to J.S. Giguere's temperamental groin problem, Reimer got his chance to crack the lineup, and he has succeeded…in spades.

There has been an unintended victim of Reimer's success. Jonas Gustavsson's role this year was to be backup to Giguere. Unfortunately, everything went off the rails for Jonas. By the end of the first quarter of the schedule, he had been the winning goalie in only 3 games, while losing 5. At the end of November, his losses had climbed to 8. One month later, that losing total spiked to 14. To make things even worse, the team appeared to have lost confidence in Gustavsson, and he seemed to lose confidence in himself. Brian Burke and his management team will now face a decision about what role, if any, Jonas will play with the Leafs next season.

The Leafs beat a spunky team last night. I wouldn't call it a pretty win, but the boys got the job done. The Leaf scorers in this one were Kulemin (2), Bozak, and Kessel. Colorado's markers came from Winnick, O'Reilly, and Duchene.

The Leafs now face a huge test on Saturday night when they meet the Detroit Red Wings on the road. Nothing has changed. They've gotta win! Yet another reality has emerged. The Leafs need some help. Some teams have got to beat the other contenders for the final Eastern Conference playoff spot. If Buffalo and Carolina keep winning, the Leafs will not prevail. They're still in the hunt, but the trail is starting to get cold.

Keep up the good work, boys! Go, Leafs…GO!

The Math Has Reached the Ugly Stage

I was afraid that this might happen. The regular season is slowly, inexorably dwindling to an end. A handful of teams in both conferences are fighting for survival. They all need wins badly.

The problem that each of these marginal teams face is this. Sooner or later, they will have to face opponents who are simply better than they are. That's why the Leafs failed to pick up a point last night at the Joe Louis Arena in Detroit. The Red Wings are better than the Leafs. They have made the playoffs for 20 years in a row. The Leafs have failed to make the playoffs for six in a row. This season, the Leafs have accumulated 78 points. The Red Wings now hold 97. The Leafs are young and inexperienced. The Red Wings are grizzled veterans.

The Leafs did not play particularly well last night. They turned the puck over to the Wings far too many times. They were not very successful in taking face-offs. Many of the shots that they took at the Detroit net were deflected away by a sea of red uniforms worn by a squadron of players who have been thoroughly schooled in the art of defensive hockey. When the Leafs managed to penetrate their zone, all five Detroit skaters came back to help their goalie fend off the attacks. In the Toronto goal, Jamie Reimer played reasonably well, but he was unable to withstand the Detroit onslaught. He definitely misplayed the shot that Hudler notched as the game-winner.

Detroit's goals were scored by Zetterberg, Holmstrom, Hudler, and Bertuzzi (into an empty net). Nazem Kadri and Joffrey Lupul replied for Toronto.

The chances of Toronto making the playoffs as this is written are purely mathematical. They have six games remaining. ***They have to win them all.***   Even if they do, that may not be enough. The other teams fighting for the eighth playoff spot, namely Buffalo and Carolina, are NOT losing their games. Next Tuesday, Buffalo visits Toronto for the last time this season. If the Sabres win, that spells curtains for the Maple Leafs, for sure!

As the final buzzer sounded at the Joe last night, the television camera panned the Maple Leaf bench. I spotted one sole Leaf player whose head was sadly shaking from left to right, and the expression on his face pretty well conveyed all that was needed.

The Leafs needed this game.

They didn't get it.

That loss was the proverbial handwriting on the wall.

The math is genuinely UGLY!

A Churchillian Victory: Winnie Would Be Proud!

... "we shall fight on the beaches, we shall fight on the landing grounds, we shall fight in the fields and in the street, we shall fight in the hills; we shall never surrender!"
- Winston Churchill - June 4, 1940

I was reminded of these unforgettable words during the course of the game last night between the Maple Leafs and the Sabres. I was overwhelmed with the sense of desperation that seemed to be driving the Leafs in this particular game. Their determination was palpable. At no point in the entire game did I ever feel that defeat was a possibility. Even after Carl Gunnarsson fumbled a clearing attempt that resulted in a tying goal being scored by Rob Niedermayer, I had a feeling that the Leafs would prevail in the long run.

Sure enough, just a few minutes later, Mikhail Grabovski, aided by Phil Kessel and Clarke MacArthur, scored what proved to be the winning goal for the home team.

This was a dandy game to watch. Both teams played extremely well. Miller and Reimer are both top-notch goalies, and they both played valiantly.

Nazem Kadri, with two points last night, is beginning to show the brilliance that we all knew he possessed and demonstrated repeatedly throughout his outstanding Junior career with the London Knights. He definitely needed to hone his skills for several months in the AHL with the Marlies, however, I doubt that any further time need be spent by Nazem in the minors. He looks just fine, thank you very much, as he helps his Leaf team-mates stave off elimination as the season winds down.

I want to pay special tribute to Clarke MacArthur after his excellent work in last night's match. Clarke had a three-point night. As this is written, Clarke has scored 21 goals and has 40 assists for a total of 61 points. He will be 26 years old in about a week's time. He has a terrific, positive attitude. He has suited up for every Leaf game this season. This young man deserves a multi-year contract, based upon his production statistics aided and abetted by his work ethic. Clarke is one of the positive elements in a Leaf season that needs to recognize <u>every</u> positive that has emerged from an environment replete with disappointments.

In addition to MacArthur and Grabovski, the other two Leaf markers were contributed by Phaneuf and Boyce. The Buffalo goals, other than the one mentioned above, were scored by Vanek and Pominville.

Tomorrow, the Leafs meet the Boston Bruins for the final time this season. The Leafs beat the Bruins just a week and a half ago, so we know that the Beantowners CAN be beaten, even though they have just nicely clinched a spot in the first round of playoff action. The Leafs can win again by playing inspired hockey, just like they did last night.

Determination Wins the Day...Again

Today is indeed April 1ˢᵗ...April Fool's Day. However, **I am not fooling! The Leafs DID win the game against the Bruins last night!**

This game, like most of the matches played by the boys in blue and white lately, had everything needed to qualify as a crowd-pleaser. The goaltending was good at both ends of the ice. There were some very good defensive plays executed by both sides. There were plenty of goals...a penalty shot...and very good goaltending again when the shootout phase of the game was played out.

That was when the Leafs had a bit of an edge on the home team. James Reimer continued his outstanding work in the Leaf net, and in the shootout, young Nazem Kadri made two or three excellent moves on Tim Thomas, and put the puck high into the net on Timmy's glove side. Game over! Another savior marker to extend the Leaf season.

At last, Joffrey Lupul got a few breaks in this match, and was able to produce three points (2 goals and 1 assist) for the first time since joining the Leafs. He has deserved this achievement for quite some time now. He has worked hard, and has said over and over again how much he likes being a Leaf, and how much he genuinely wants to help his team improve.

Congratulations are also due to both Luke Schenn and Phil Kessel. These two guys contributed two points each to last night's heroics. I hope that Kessel realizes that assists are every bit as valuable as goals when it comes to a team producing winning performances.

Nazem Kadri has arrived as a Leaf. He has been chosen as one of the three stars in three of the past six Leaf matches. He was the only scorer of the six in last night's shootout. I'm sure that his marker, that beat Thomas cleanly, made him a hero in the eyes of his team-mates. The way that they celebrated at the end of the game was as joyous as any that we've witnessed all season.

Lupul...Schenn...Kadri...Reimer...the list goes on and on...! These kids are closing out this season in a virtual blaze of glory! What tremendous hope they are inspiring within the Leaf nation!

They must not let up! They must press on! There are FOUR games remaining, and it astonishes us to realize that they STILL have not been eliminated. The Leafs genuinely do not want to be eliminated, either. You can see that by the way that they're playing.

Leaf hockey is fun again! Keep it up, boys!

Go, Leafs...Go, Go, Go!

Leafs Overpower Sens for Critical Victory

They did it again! Last night, the near-capacity crowd at Ottawa's Scotiabank Place was privileged to see a very spirited game, yet another tilt in the Battle of Ontario. There were many in attendance that were there to support the Maple Leafs in their struggle to make the playoffs. They were not to be disappointed. The Leafs continued to play hard against their opponents, absolutely refusing to give ground to any and all who seek to banish them to another unrewarding season, on the outside, looking in.

Bozak, Kadri, Kulemin, and Kessel all fired shots that beat Craig Anderson, the Senators' new goalie. Anderson has certainly made a good impression in the nation's capital since he arrived there from Colorado. The team's management has been so impressed that they have signed him to a multi-year contract. He will be their main goalie when training camp assembles next September.

Phil Kessel opened the scoring with his 30th goal of the season. Phil is 23 years of age, and is completing his fifth season as a big-leaguer. For the past three campaigns, he has scored 36, 30, and 30 goals. respectively. There is little doubt that he has justified the high cost that Brian Burke paid to acquire his services. As he continues to mature as a player, his natural skill set should make him realize an even higher level of success than he has attained thus far in a fine career.

Nazem Kadri proved again last night that we can expect a high level of achievement from him over the next few years. After spending the bulk of the season homing his skills with the Marlies in the AHL, he appears to be improving as an NHLer every game out. Bozak's marker was his fifteenth, and Kulemin's his 29th this year. Both of these players appear to have promising futures with the Leaf organization.

In the net, James Reimer's win against the Senators has to be regarded as a landmark. Four months ago, few people knew much, if anything, about him. Last night, he chalked up his twentieth game as the winning goaltender. History will record him as the Leaf's Number One goalie this season. His ascent to stardom has been spectacular. His superlative play can be credited as the main source of inspiration for his team-mates in their drive for the post-season.

In five more days, the Leafs will have completed their regular season schedule. Tomorrow night, they will host the Washington Capitals. On Wednesday, they travel to New Jersey. Then, on Saturday night, the finale will feature a visit by the Montreal Canadiens. The Leafs MUST win all three of these games. Even then, their chances of success are miniscule.

Win or lose, the effort that they have mustered has been fantastic.

Maple Leafs Eliminated from Playoffs

It's over! Everything is official now. The 2010 – 2011 hockey season will end for the Leafs as the final buzzer sounds on Saturday night at the Air Canada Centre.

The Toronto Maple Leaf schedule began on October 1st of 2010 with the team facing off against their long-time rivals, the Montreal Canadiens. It will conclude three days from now with those same two teams competing. Sadly, there will be nothing at stake for the home team. **For the SIXTH consecutive season, there will not be a single post-season game played at the Air Canada Centre…the mecca of hockey in the minds of legions of fans.**

THE TRUTH OF THAT SENTENCE IS ABSOLUTELY DISGRACEFUL

Forty-four years without a Stanley Cup win. Six straight years of playoff elimination. Failure upon failure upon failure. I have watched it all unfurl for decades. It is heart-wrenching, and VERY difficult to absorb. When will it all end?

The team fought valiantly once again last night, but it was all for naught. The out-of-town scoreboard flashed the news that the Buffalo Sabres had defeated the Tampa Bay Lightning, and that victory put an end to any hope of the Leafs playing beyond Saturday night.

There were two positives that can be gleaned from this game by the home club. James Reimer played another outstanding game, stopping 39 of the 41 shots leveled at him by the Capitals through a full 65 minutes of regulation time and overtime. After one particularly brilliant sequence of saves in the third period, the crowd rose to their feet and gave him a standing, screaming ovation. I hope that he enjoyed it. He richly deserved each and every cheer!

The second positive factor last night was the fact that Nicolai Kulemin scored his 30th goal of the season. This young man is one of the more promising players on the Leaf roster. He is still a kid, and should have several more successful years in a blue and white uniform.

The Washington victory moved that team into first place in the Eastern Conference, and it certainly was a morale-boosting event in advance of the first round of playoff action.

Tonight, the Leafs will face the Devils in New Jersey. Reimer will be given the night off. I hope that the team plays well. I will understand it though, if they drop this game. They must be both tired and disappointed after playing with such courage and dedication over the past few weeks. Alas, it was too little…too late.

Devils Prevail Over Feisty Leaf Crew

The Maple Leafs skated out against the New Jersey Devils last night a tired and disappointed bunch of players. This was their second game in as many nights, but, most significant of all was the reality of their elimination from the playoffs less than twenty-four hours earlier.

As has been the case so many times this season, the Leafs dug themselves into a hole and didn't have the juice to get themselves out of it. The Devils, also out of the playoffs, readily volunteered after the game that their motivation remains fairly high for a couple of reasons. First of all, if they win all of their remaining games, they can record a winning record for the year. After a terrible start, followed by a coaching change, that will give them a measure of satisfaction. Secondly, if they beat the New York Rangers in their final game, they could become the deciding factor about whether the Rangers or Carolina claim the final playoff spot in the Eastern Conference.

The only goal of the first period was scored by Ilya Kovalchuk. It was his 30th goal of the season...a very important milestone in any hockey player's career. Tedenby and Tallinder added goals for the Devils in the second period, and the Leafs skated off to the second intermission facing almost certain defeat.

If there were any over-riding questions going through my mind at that point in the match, they were:

Why in the name of #$%@%^& was Reimer playing goal in this game?

Why, after the exhausting style of hockey that he has played game after game, was he not permitted to rest up for the final game on Saturday?

Why was Giguere, who, after all, is getting paid several million dollars this year, not insisting that he give his 23 year old counterpart a bit of a break?

Only Ron Wilson can give you an answer to those questions. To me, and to many of the media who commented upon the situation, it was a no-brainer that Reimer needed and deserved a break. Wilson's decision to play him just reinforces my belief that a coaching change in September is needed. More on that later.

The Leafs played much better in the final period. Phil Kessel scored his 31st of the season, and then Tyler Bozak notched a short-handed goal with Phaneuf in the penalty box. Unfortunately, Elias scored into an empty net, and that proved to be the insurance goal that the Devils needed.

The Leaf season will come to an end on Saturday evening at the Air Canada Centre, when they take on the playoff-bound Montreal Canadiens. It would be great if the Leafs could end the schedule with a win over the bleu, blanc, et rouge.

Leafs Unable to Match Playoff-Bound Habs

Another sad chapter in Toronto Maple Leaf history came to an end last night with the team falling to a much sharper Montreal opponent. After all of the exciting hockey that we watched as the Leafs valiantly tried to get to the post-season, this one was a disappointment. In addition to closing out their season with a win, it is worthwhile to note that this contest marked the 600th victory for head coach Jacques Martin, of the Canadiens. The Canadiens will meet the Boston Bruins in the first playoff round, beginning next Thursday.

Both goalies played well last night, but it was Carey Price in the Montreal net who prevailed on this occasion. He has had a very good season, and appears very ready to backstop his team against a very imposing Bruin squad. It should be a dandy series to watch.

The Montreal goals were scored by Ryan White, Brian Gionta, with two, and Tomas Plekanec. Phil Kessel scored the only Toronto marker, his 32nd of the schedule. His goal was assisted by Joe Colborne, called up from the Marlies to appear in his very first NHL game. He looks like a very promising candidate for a future Leaf team. He is a big boy, who can be expected to put more beef on his frame, and is reputed to have some important offensive skills at his disposal. Another call-up last night was Matt Frattin, and he played very well when given some ice time in this game.

All in all, this was not a very well-played game by the home squad, no doubt the result of being eliminated from the playoffs earlier in the week. At the final buzzer, the Leafs all skated out onto the ice, and waited as the Canadiens congratulated Price for his fine effort and skated to their dressing room. The Leafs then all raised their sticks skyward in a salute to their fans, a gesture of thanks for the strong support that this team always receives, no matter how badly things seem to turn out.

So, dear readers, the Leaf season is over...once again, far too soon. Of course, I will continue to follow the playoffs closely, taking particular interest in the series that will feature the Canadian clubs that remain in contention. Sadly, FOUR of the Canadian teams have fallen by the wayside. In addition to the Leafs, the Ottawa Senators, Calgary Flames, and Edmonton Oilers failed to advance. I will cheer for Montreal, in the Eastern Conference and Vancouver in the West. It looks very much like the Vancouver Canucks, who literally ran away from the pack in the Western Conference, have a very good chance to win the Stanley Cup this year. We'll see. There is an awful lot of hockey yet to be played, and we all know that weird things happen as the playoffs advance.

Over the course of the next few days, I will summarize the Leaf season in considerable detail, and outline my expectations for next season. Stay tuned!

April 11, 2011

The Maple Leaf Season Reviewed

What Happened?

The Leaf Season at a Glance

The line graph shown above is an accurate visual record of all 82 games played by the Leafs this season. To make this graph, I used a statistic that I call the team's "Winning Percentage". Following each game, I divided the team's total points earned by the total points possible. That answer gave me the winning percentage figure.

The season began on October 1st. The Leafs posted four straight wins. Everything was sweetness and light!

Then…catastrophe! The Leafs went on a losing streak in which they won just a single game…**AND LOST ELEVEN!** Their winning percentage had plummeted to 40.5. That losing streak cost the Leafs a place in the playoffs. In a league as competitive as the present-day NHL, a team simply cannot lose eleven out of twelve games and expect to compete in the post-season. The gap is simply too big to close.

The graph trends upward following the team's cataclysmic plunge, but, no matter how hard the players tried, they never even got back to the 60 percent mark for the remainder of the season.

Of course, there were several significant factors that contributed to the team's troubles. Among them were:

1. A major injury to Team Captain Dion Phaneuf. He sustained a very deep cut to the back of his left leg, and was out of action for the entire month of November. Even after he returned, we will never be able to know how long it actually took for him to regain all the strength that the injury cost him. Tough players like Phaneuf rarely disclose the total damage that they sustain from injuries, and they frequently play through a lot of pain. Phaneuf's absence also left a leadership gap on the club, because nobody else stepped up and took the responsibility normally expected of a captain. Beauchemin, Komisarek, and Kaberle wore the "A" on their jerseys, but none of them exercised the captain's role with any conviction or competence.

2. Colby Armstrong's injuries, both at the beginning and at the end of the season, cost the Leafs the services of a feisty, effective player. He was only able to suit up for 50 games this year, and his absence was sorely felt. Colby has a high energy level of performance.

He is pugnacious, and unafraid to engage the opponent with vigour and aggression. The team missed him very much when he was unable to play.

3. Jonas Gustavsson's season can now be officially classified as a disaster. By the end of December, he had been the losing goaltender in 14 games.

    On January 19th, the Maple Leafs lost to the New York Rangers by a score of 7 – 0. Gustavsson was in the net for more than 53 minutes of that game, and was tagged as the losing goaltender. On the charts that I keep for research purposes, I have highlighted that match in red, indicating that it may well have been the worst Leaf performance of the season. It turned out to be Gustavsson's final appearance in the net this season. He had lost the confidence of his team-mates, but most importantly, he lost his own self-confidence. By the end of the season, he was dressed only occasionally in a backup role, and at one point was officially demoted to the Marlies in the AHL. In addition, he had suffered some more heart problems, and needed another procedure called an ablation repeated for the third time since becoming a Leaf. At this writing, his future in the Maple Leaf organization is in doubt. It is possible that we may never see him in the Leaf net again.

4. Phil Kessel had an abysmal scoring drought midway through the season. Although he eventually came out of it, and had a successful season, his scoring woes definitely didn't help the team, and their ability to develop a consistent attack was hampered. Rightly or wrongly, Kessel has been designated by Brian Burke as the cornerstone of the Maple Leaf hockey club. While there is no doubt that he is a highly skilled player, it is also clear that he needs much more support around him that Burke has been able to supply to this point in his regime. I will have more to say about both Burke and Kessel later in this work.

Assessing the Management Team

These are the people who comprise the Management Team of the Toronto Maple Leafs:

Brian Burke	President & General Manager
Dave Nonis	Senior Vice-President – Hockey Operations
Dave Poulin	Vice-President – Hockey Operations
Claude Loiselle	Assistant General Manager
Cliff Fletcher	Senior Adviser
Jim Hughes	Director of Player Development
Reid Mitchell	Director, Hockey & Scouting Administration
Dave Griffiths	Team Services Manager

Brian Burke assumed his present role as President and General Manager of the Toronto Maple Leafs on November 29, 2008. As we are all aware, he inherited a team that was in total disarray. Burke brought with him a long and distinguished career in the National Hockey

League. It was clear from the very day that he assumed his position as Leaf GM that this was going to be **HIS** team in every sense of the word.

Brian Burke has a Stanley Cup ring. He earned it as General Manager of the Anaheim Ducks, when they captured the trophy in 2007. Essentially, his mission, as I see it, is to bring another Stanley Cup to Toronto.

Nothing else matters. Burke's management team surrounds him with a cadre of smart hockey men. Several are people with whom he has worked in the past, or else are associated with his alma mater, Providence College. He also has a long association with Head Coach Ron Wilson. It is apparent that Burke places a high premium on loyalty, and there are strong indicators in the Leaf organization that loyalty is regarded as a two-way street.

As far as rendering an accurate assessment of the management team, it is still far too early in their tenure to do so. Rebuilding this particular team was never viewed by anyone to be a short-term process. However, Burke is keenly aware that expectations are high. I honestly believe that he thought that this year's team was capable of making the playoffs. The fact that they didn't will motivate him even more as he and the team move in the off-season to strengthen the club in preparation for next season. Failing to make the playoffs next year is simply not an option. If that happens, it could spell the end of his tenure in Toronto. In his end-of-the-season media conference, Burke made it very clear that he regarded this season as a failure, but at the same time he commended several specific players for helping the team to a strong second half. He promised to continue that trend in 2011 – 2012.

I am confident that he will spare no effort to keep that promise.

Assessing the Coaching Staff

The list that follows here identifies each member of the Maple Leaf coaching staff and their responsibilities:

Ron Wilson	Head Coach
Keith Acton	Assistant Coach
Tim Hunter	Assistant Coach
Rob Zettler	Assistant Coach
Francois Allaire	Goaltending Coach
Graeme Townshend	Skating Coach
Chris Dennis	Video Coach

At the outset, I want to state that I am unable to comment upon the work of Graeme Townshend or Chris Dennis. Their work is performed well out of the public view, and, in my opinion has little direct impact on the final results recorded by the team as a whole. I concur that both of these gentlemen might not agree with that statement, but, let's face it, when things go wrong, as they have this season, the heat does not initially get focused upon the skating or video coaches. They probably do their very best in carrying out their responsibilities, and I am certainly in no position to even suggest otherwise.

The same can be said about Francois Allaire. Over time, I have read and heard enough about Mr. Allaire to know that he has earned a very favourable reputation in NHL circles as a goalie coach. If Brian Burke decides to retain Francois' services with next year's team, I have absolutely no problem supporting Mr. Allaire's tenure.

I have a major problem with the matter of retaining the other four coaches.

While I am not calling for Ron Wilson's firing, <u>I am strongly advocating his replacement as Head Coach.</u>

In his post-season comments, Brian Burke has stated quite openly that he is NOT going to fire Ron Wilson, and that Wilson, along with whatever support staff he wants, will be back in September for another kick at the cat. I sincerely hope that such a scenario does **NOT** happen.

An ideal scenario, in my mind, anyway, would see Ron Wilson deciding to **retire** as Head Coach.

<u>I don't want Ron Wilson to be fired.</u> He doesn't deserve that fate. He is a very accomplished NHL coach with more than 600 wins to his credit, and has earned far too much respect to be treated with such indignity. If Ron was to simply retire, there would be nothing to impede Burke from appointing him as another member of the management team as a Senior Advisor, either replacing or joining the group as an equal partner to Cliff Fletcher.

As presently constituted, the Toronto Maple Leafs is one of the youngest teams in the National Hockey League. Ron Wilson is 56 years of age. That reality separates him from his charges by an age gap <u>of nearly two generations.</u> I submit, dear readers, that such a gap is too much. A young team, in my view, needs a younger coach than Ron Wilson...someone to whom the players could relate more closely.

Dallas Eakins, currently serving as Head Coach of the Marlies, has been with the Leaf organization for several years now. If he has been groomed as a future Leaf coach, then I would suggest that he be promoted NOW. Next season is critical, and it seems logical to me that a young team, led by a younger Head Coach would be more likely to get the job done.

Let's face it, folks. The Ron Wilson regime in Toronto has NOT been successful. Ron has coached for three years, and the team has not made the playoffs. At the worst and lowest point this season, the ACC fans were literally screaming for his head on a platter. "Fire Wilson! Fire Wilson!" The screams reverberating through the Air Canada Centre were echoed everywhere in the media. The team was playing poorly. The power play was ineffective. Penalty killing was a joke. On MANY occasions, I could see little, if anything, suggesting that the club was being coached with any competence. Imaginative strategies or innovation were nowhere to be seen. In my view, the time for change has arrived.

If Eakins is really the heir apparent to the head coaching position, I urge Mr. Burke to appoint him as soon as it is expedient. Let Eakins name his own assistants, and start the planning process for next season at once.

In summary, I view the present coaching situation as inadequate, and I see nothing that would suggest that Wilson and his staff merit any thought of contract extensions. Burke's loyalty to his friend is admirable, but I believe that common sense suggests that the time for change has arrived.

Perhaps the MLSE Board of Directors should consider imposing a bit of common sense into the situation…but only as a last resort. I honestly believe that Brian Burke should carry the can for all the changes required for success in 2011 – 2012.

Assessing the Players

Three Star Selections

We are all familiar with the long-standing tradition in the NHL of naming three players at the conclusion of each game who have performed with excellence. One of the charts that I devised to help me tell the story of this year's Maple Leaf team compiled a game-by-game tally of the players whose performances carried the club throughout the season.

My chart clearly shows that three players dominated the three-star selections this year. Those players were:

Mikhail Grabovski	18 selections
Phil Kessel	17 selections
James Reimer	13 selections

Three other players also deserve honourable mention for having been selected on many other occasions throughout the schedule. Their names are:

Nik Kulemin	8 selections
Clarke MacArthur	7 selections
Tyler Bozak	7 selections

Three star choices are obviously not as reliable criteria for evaluation purposes as other measures, but the overview of the selections gives one a general sense of the players whose contributions were consistent as the season unfolded.

To give credit where credit is due, here are the other players whose names appear on the chart and the number of times that they were chosen as game stars:

J. S. Giguere - 4	Kris Versteeg - 4
Luke Schenn - 5	Mike Komisarek - 1
Francois Beauchemin - 1	Tomas Kaberle - 5
Jonas Gustavsson - 4	Nazem Kadri - 3
Colby Armstrong - 4	Joey Crabb - 2
Dion Phaneuf - 4	Tim Brent - 3
Joffrey Lupul - 3	Darryl Boyce - 1

There were 246 stars available to be named. The Leafs claimed 114 of them. That is a winning percentage of 46.3. That is NOT good enough, and it is an accurate reflection of the way the season progressed.

Assessing the Goaltenders

Three men played goal for the Toronto Maple Leafs this season: They were:

Jean Sebastien Giguere	Age – 33
Jonas Gustavsson	Age - 26
James Reimer	Age - 23

The following chart outlines a summary of their record in terms of wins and losses:

	Game Appearances	Wins	Losses
Giguere	33	11	15
Gustavsson	23	6	15
Reimer	37	**20**	15

Finally, this chart records some other stats that have significance in terms of evaluating goaltender performances:

	Giguere	Gustavsson	Reimer
Minutes Played	1633	1242	2080
Goals Against	78	68	90
Goals Against Ave.	2.87	3.29	**2.60**
Shutouts	0	0	**3**
Saves	777	620	1134
Save Percentage	.900	.890	**.921**

"The best laid schemes o 'mice and Men Gang aft a-gley;
And leave us naught but grief and pain
For promised joy."

Robbie Burns

Those words of the great Scottish poet certainly sum up what happened in terms of goaltending for the Toronto Maple Leafs in 2010 – 2011. The original plan for the goalies was that Jean Sebastien Giguere would begin the season as the main starting goalie. He was 33 years of age, was being paid the princely amount of $ 7,000,000 and had close to 600 games under his belt in the NHL.

Giguere would also serve as a mentor to his backup, Jonas Gustavsson, a young man of 26 from Sweden who had been hotly pursued by several NHL clubs before signing with Toronto in 2009. Following his initial year with the Leafs, he signed a two-year contract in the summer of 2010 that would pay him an average salary of $ 1.35 million per annum. Jonas was considered to be the heir apparent to the Leaf goaltending starter's position. He would gradually transition to that status as the season progressed.

That plan didn't work out.

We all remember how, after a terrific start to the season that saw the team win their first four games, the wheels fell off the bus, and the Leafs plunged down the standings to the point that they almost lost hope of contending for the playoffs. By the end of December, the Leafs had a record of only 13 wins and 19 losses.

Giguere had 5 of those losses, and was experiencing groin problems that seriously hampered his mobility when playing.

Gustavsson was named the winning goalie in just 5 games, and the loser in 14. The team had become notorious for being scored upon early in many matches, forcing them into situations where they had to come from behind time and time again. More often than not, this was impossible. Jonas was guilty of giving up more than his share of "soft" goals. He soon lost the confidence of his team-mates, but worse than that, he appeared to lose confidence in himself. His 15th, and final loss of the season came on January 19th against the New York Rangers. We never saw Jonas in the Leaf net after that game.

Jonas Gustavsson's woes did not end there. After being assigned to the Toronto Marlies for conditioning, and hopefully the restoration of his self-confidence, he suffered a medical setback. Jonas apparently has a tricky heart. On two occasions during the 2009 – 2010 season, he needed a procedure known as an ablation to correct an irregular heartbeat. During his assignment to the Marlies, he needed another. Talk about bad luck! To sum things up… Jonas has had a very disheartening season…no pun intended.

Meanwhile, back at the ranch, a young man named James Reimer rode to the rescue of the Toronto Maple Leafs. Recalled from the Toronto Marlies of the AHL, with his meager contract for $ 550,000 safely tucked into his bank account, this 23 year-old kid from Manitoba arrived upon the scene. In the time since his arrival, and first appearance in the Leaf net on December 20th, **James Reimer has laid claim to the ownership of the primary Leaf goaltender's position.**

James Reimer, and his meteoric rise to goaltending success in Toronto has emerged as one of the most compelling stories in the Toronto Sports media in quite some time. At this writing, Reimer is on the cusp of being named as the starting goalie in the World Hockey Championships to be played within the next couple of weeks in Europe. That's pretty heady stuff for a kid finishing his rookie year in the NHL!

In summary then, where does all of this leave us.

Jamie Reimer is now THE goaltender for the Toronto Maple Leafs. That will be his status when training camp opens in September.

Jonas Gustavsson's future as a Maple Leaf is uncertain. He has a contract for next season. The management team will have to decide whether to:
a) Give him another chance to make the team as Reimer's backup,
b) Trade him to another NHL club,
c) Assign him to the Marlies of the AHL, or
d) Buy out his contract, and let him return to hockey in Europe.

Jean Sebastien Giguere's future with the Leafs is also uncertain. At his post-season media scrum, Brian Burke indicated that Giguere may need surgery in order to permanently correct his recurring groin problems. Jean's contract with the Leafs terminates at the end of June, and he will become an unrestricted free agent with a cap salary of $ 6,000,000. He is still a young man, and probably does not see himself as ready to retire, but whatever happens, he will probably have to modify his salary expectations, particularly since he has some health issues on his record.

One thing is clear. The Toronto Maple Leafs will need to address the issue of goaltending over the course of the summer. James Reimer will need to have a very reliable goalie to back him up next season. Who will that person be? Your guess is as good as mine.

Good luck, Mr. Burke!

Assessing the Maple Leaf Defence

At the conclusion of this season, there were seven players listed on the Leaf roster as defencemen. In my statistical chart (below), I am also including the two blueliners who were traded away at the February 28th trade deadline. Fraancois Beauchemin was returned to Anaheim and Tomas Kaberle is now with the Boston Bruins.

	G.P.	Goals	Assists	Points	+/-	PIM
Keith Aulie (21)	40	2	0	2	-1	32
Carl Gunnarsson (24)	68	4	16	20	-2	14
Mike Komisarek (29)	75	1	9	10	-8	86
Matt Lashoff (24)	11	0	1	1	1	6
Brett Lebda (29)	41	1	3	4	-14	14
Dion Phaneuf (26)	66	8	22	30	-2	88
Luke Schenn (21)	82	5	17	22	-7	34
Francois Beauchemin (30)	*54*	*2*	*10*	*12*	*NA*	*16*
Tomas Kaberle (33)	*58*	*3*	*35*	*38*	*NA*	*16*
TOTALS		**26**	**113**	**139**		

The defensive corps of the Toronto Maple Leafs did NOT have a successful year. The team **was scored upon 48 more times than the entire club scored against the opposition.** All Eastern Conference teams that made the playoffs posted a positive difference between goals for and against. The greatest differential was **Boston's + 51**, and the smallest was **a tie between Montreal and Tampa Bay with + 7**.

The two departed defenders, Beauchemin and Kaberle, were both veterans of long standing in the NHL. I never had the sense that Beauchemin was comfortable in Toronto. To me, he was a decent, soft-spoken sort of guy who, in my opinion, could have played a lot better than he did. He could have been more assertive with many of his younger team-mates than he was. After returning to Anaheim, from whence he came, he made a statement to the media that he wished that he hadn't sold his house after his trade to Toronto. That comment caused me to question his enthusiasm for that trade in the first place. Perhaps his trade to the Leafs was at least a minor mistake on Brian Burke's part. We'll maybe never know.

Tomas Kaberle became a multi-millionaire as a Toronto Maple Leaf. He benefitted from a long-term contract, complete with a no-trade clause in his final few years as a Leaf. It was only when he waived his no-trade clause that Burke was finally able to deal him to Boston. Frankly, for the last couple of years, it mystified me why he wanted to play in Toronto, because it was obvious that he did not play a large part in the club's future plans. At the beginning of training camp last September, he even suffered the indignity of having coach Ron Wilson deny him the role of Assistant Captain, although it was restored later in the season, when Captain Dion Phaneuf was injured.

I certainly viewed Kaberle as a better-than-average defenceman, but never a superstar. An excellent skater, and very skilled at getting the puck transitioned from defence to offence, I would rank his offensive talents slightly higher than his defensive skills. To support my contention, I submit that his average scoring output of almost a half-point per game, consistent throughout his career as a Leaf is far better than most blueliners. Even though he was a fairly productive player, he frequently exasperated me by passing the puck to one or more of his team-mates, rather than taking shots at the net himself.

After the trade deadline at the end of February, both Beauchemin and Kaberle had been dispatched out of the country, one to the west coast of the USA and the other to the east. Sixty-three years had been subtracted from the Maple Leaf defensive corps. Not a single remaining defender was older than 29

The two oldest remaining Leaf defenders were Brett Lebda and Mike Komisarek, both of whom were 29. As bad luck would have it, both players fell victim to injuries in their first years with the Leafs.

Last season, Komisarek was only able to play 34 games. Although he was injury-free throughout this season, his performance level was not up to the expectations that both management and the media had for him. He was also guilty of taking some questionably penalties. These factors resulted in diminished ice time. At one point, there was some speculation that the injury which he suffered in 2009 – 2010 caused him to be a bit "gun-shy" this year. At any rate, his play improved in the later stages of the season, and he ended the campaign on a fairly positive note.

On a personal note, I have always had a good impression about Mike. He seems to be very personable in most of the media scrums that I have seen on television. It would appear that he has a good sense of humour, and might well be a bit of a prankster on occasion. He was one of the Leaf assistant captains this year, and on a couple of occasions, when the team had faltered, he appeared in front of the television cameras, and spoke candidly about why his team-mates had come up short. I hope that Mike can put together a really good season in 2011 – 2012. He is a hard worker, and deserves a goodly share of success.

When the Leafs acquired Brett Lebda from Detroit, they knew that they were getting a solid, veteran defenceman. He won a Stanley Cup ring with the Red Wings, and he is certainly able to impress upon his younger colleagues the necessity for hard, diligent work if they want to achieve the ultimate prize in professional hockey. Although his injury hampered him in his initial season with the Leafs, he got some substantial ice time in the later stages of the campaign. He will be counted upon to play a major role on the team next year.

Dion Phaneuf has had a very rough first full season as a Maple Leaf. On November 2nd, in a loss to provincial rival Ottawa Senators, Dion sustained a very serious cut to the back of his left leg. It was a very deep cut, and had to be surgically repaired. It was first announced that Dion would miss between four and six weeks of play. He returned to action on November 28, and hindsight tells me that he came back too soon. Phaneuf took a lot of media heat in the middle stretch of the season. He was not putting up the numbers expected of him. His style of play was less robust than usual. He was not as forceful a leader as he was expected to be in his role as team captain. It was even suggested that he had been named captain before he had really earned the position.

I felt at the time, and I STILL DO, that these shots in the media were grossly unfair to Dion. Only he, and perhaps a couple of the training staff members, will ever know the true toll that the cut he suffered really took on him. I believe that a cut that was as severe as the one he suffered takes a long time to heal completely. I am willing to bet money that Phaneuf returned to play before he really should have. Professional athletes are notorious for playing hurt, and I am reasonably certain that Dion played hurt for several weeks following his return to the team. I offer his modest numbers as evidence of that. Furthermore, the record clearly shows significantly improved numbers in the final weeks of the campaign (12 points in March).

Luke Schenn had a terrific year. He has played for the Leafs for three complete seasons, and I believe that he is getting markedly better with each passing year. This kid is still just 21 years old, yet he is acknowledged as one of the best players on the team. In the three years on the Leafs, Luke's penalty minutes number 71, 50, and 34. To me, those figures indicate that he is performing at an increasingly high level, while at the same time taking fewer penalties to do so. In other words, he is becoming a more proficient and efficient player. This year, Luke was 8th highest in the NHL with 251 hits registered. He also blocked 186 shots with his body. In addition to his stellar playing, he consistently gives a large amount of money through the year to his "Luke's Troops" initiative which allows military personnel to attend Leaf home games at the Air Canada Centre. Luke is an outstanding Leaf player...a wonderful example to all young people in every walk of life.

The other three defenders can all be described as "hot prospects" for future Leaf teams. They are all in their early twenties. Matt Lashoff spent most of the season with the Marlies. He was a late call-up in the final few games of the schedule. He should be given a good opportunity to make the club in training camp. We got a good look at both Carl Gunnarsson and Keith Aulie this year, and I was very impressed with their skills as blueliners. Based upon their work this year, I would venture the opinion that both of these young men are almost sure-fire bets to make next year's Leaf squad.

In terms of evaluating the overall contribution of this year's defensive corps to the entire production of the team, I would have to say that it was below par. In my view, I would expect a team's total production to be comprised as follows:

Centres	25%
Left Wing	25%
Right Wing	25%
Defence	25%

This year's Maple Leaf defencemen contributed only **22%** of the team's total scoring. The Washington Capitals, finishing 1st in the Eastern Conference, got **26%** of their team's production from the defenders.

My analysis of the statistics revealed by the charts that I keep throughout the season leads me to conclude that a 4% improvement in the work of the defence would have at least allowed the Leafs to get into the post-season. While I have, on occasion, heard NHL defencemen argue that they are getting paid good money to **defend**, it would be my contention that their overall responsibility would consist of 75% defence...but 25% offence. Contributions to the team's attack from the blue line are indispensable.

Assessing the Centre Ice Position

In order to be successful in the National Hockey League, a team MUST be strong "down the middle". Hockey teams are constructed in such a way that there are FOUR forward lines. Common sense dictates that there needs to be at least TWO of those lines that present genuine scoring threats to opposing teams. If the scoring production of any team can be distributed among six or seven forwards, then such a team cannot be shut down by having opposition defenders focus upon a single line.

This year, the centre position proved to be the "Achilles Heel" of the Toronto Maple Leafs. They were not strong at that position when the season began, and they are still not strong there as the team looks forward to training camp in September.

Eight players performed at centre ice for the Leafs in 2010 – 2011.

	GP	Goals	Assists	Points	+/	PIM
Mikhail Grabovski (27)	81	29	29	58	14	60
Tyler Bozak (25)	82	15	17	32	-29	14
Nazem Kadri (20)	29	3	9	12	-3	8
Tim Brent (27)	79	8	12	20	-4	33
Joe Colborne (21)	1	0	1	1	1	0
Mike Zigomanis (30)	8	0	1	1	0	4
Christian Hanson (25	6	0	0	0	0	4
Marcel Mueller (22)	3	0	0	0	0	2
TOTALS		**55**	**69**	**124**		

I will begin my evaluation of the centremen by commenting about the four players whose contributions to this year's Leaf team were minimal.

Marcel Mueller did not make the team in training camp. He appeared in only three NHL games, but spent almost all of the season with the Marlies. There, he had a mediocre record of 14 goals and 19 assists, for 33 points in 57 games.

Christian Hanson was another player who was not able to stick with the parent club. He was, like Mueller, assigned to the Marlies where he posted a very similar scoring record (13 + 21 = 34) with the Leafs' AHL affiliate.

Joe Colborne was called up to the Leafs for a single game to give him a chance to experience life in the NHL. He is a big kid who has made a good impression with the Marlies after being acquired by Brian Burke as part of the Kaberle trade. He shows considerable promise for future Leaf teams.

Mike Zigomanis is a well-travelled professional hockey player. In the NHL, he has played with FIVE teams, those being Pittsburgh Penguins, Phoenix Coyotes, St. Louis Blues, Carolina Hurricane, and the Leafs. He picked up a Stanley Cup ring in 2009, while playing for the Pittsburgh Penguins. Mike's contract with the Leafs was a two-way arrangement, so he was assigned to the Marlies, where he had a fairly good season, scoring 14 goals and 33 assists, for 47 points.

I will always be puzzled why Zigomanis was not given a decent chance to play with the Leafs this season. He possesses skills in the area of penalty killing, and Lord knows the Leafs didn't do very well in that department in 2010 – 2011. The fact that he assisted on 33 goals with the Marlies suggests to me that he also possesses set-up capabilities that the parent club could have used. I am inclined to feel that Mike's talents could have been better used by the Leafs, rather than being wasted with the Marlies.

Tim Brent has had a very successful year with the Maple Leafs. He showed himself to be a hard worker. He contributed very well to the penalty-killing function of the team. He scored several important goals over the course of the season. It would have been interesting to see how well he could have combined with a guy like Zigomanis. Even though they are both centremen, Brent is young enough to adapt to a key role elsewhere on the ice. Oh, well!

I am willing to predict a very bright future for Nazem Kadri with the Toronto Maple Leafs. He was a genuine superstar in Junior Hockey, and I believe that he has the same potential in the NHL. He was definitely not ready for the Leafs in the Fall, and undoubtedly benefitted from spending the bulk of the season with the Marlies. With the AHL club, he posted 41 points in 44 games. He is possibly the most talented prospect in the Maple Leaf organization at this time. Currently, he has scored 12 points in 30 NHL appearances.

Tyler Bozak played in every game this season. I view him as a very talented young player who has the potential to put up some very impressive numbers when the Leafs eventually become competitive. Thus far in his NHL career he has recorded 59 points in 119 games. That calculates to half a point per game in slightly more than one complete season. Those kinds of stats, plus the kind of potential that I feel he possesses, give rise to great optimism for Tyler's future as a big-leaguer. His +/- rating of -29 is a very misleading statistic for this past campaign. Much of his ice time was spent on the penalty kill, and that is one area of the game that this year's Leafs were less than impressive.

Mikhail Grabovski has had a career year this season as a Toronto Maple Leaf. He came within a whisker of being a thirty goal scorer, with 29 markers to his credit. He also added 29 assists to that production record for a total of 58 points. He and his line-mates Nikolai Kulemin and Clarke MacArthur formed one of Toronto's most impressive scoring threats over the course of the 2010 – 2011 campaign.

Grabovski would have joined his fellow centre ice colleague Tyler Bozak in playing all 82 games this year, save for one special event…a milestone in his life. On December 30, 2010, he was given permission to miss the game against the Columbus Blue Jackets so he could attend the birth of his daughter, whom Mikhail and his girlfriend Kate named Lily.

Grabovski's play all season long was outstanding. Many of the goals that he scored were important and game-changing. He was named as one of the three stars in EIGHTEEN games, a record that clearly identifies him as one of the top Leaf players this year. He has one more year remaining on a very lucrative Leaf contract.

So there we have it. Grabovski and Bozak carried the load at centre ice this season. The team's lack of enough strength up the middle was a weakness that hindered its progress from October right through until April. Brian Burke and his team are well aware that they must correct this shortfall in the organization over the summer. There is some reason for hope on the horizon, though. Joe Colborne has had a very auspicious start to his career in the Leaf organization, and looks like a real "comer". Burke has also acquired several good draft pick opportunities for this year's entry draft. And, who knows, the free-agent market just may offer one or two possibilities to consider.

The future could brighten considerably in the next couple of months.

Assessing the Left Wing

Skating on the left wing for the Maple Leafs in the 2010 – 2011 season were the following six individuals:

	GP	Goals	Assists	Points	+/	PIM
Clarke MacArthur (26)	82	21	41	62	-3	37
Nikolai Kulemin (24)	82	30	27	57	7	26
Darryl Boyce (26)	46	5	8	13	8	33
Fredrik Sjostrom (27)	66	2	3	5	-5	14
Jay Rosehill (25)	26	1	2	3	-6	71
Luca Caputi (22)	7	0	0	0	-2	4
TOTALS		58	81	139		

Luca Caputi appeared to have some potential as a big-leaguer in the late stages of the 2009 – 10 season and in training camp last September. Unfortunately though, the coaching staff came to the conclusion after only three regular season games that he was better suited for the American Hockey League, therefore he was dispatched to the Marlies.

Jay Rosehill was another player in the Leaf system whose season was divided between the Marlies and the Leafs. When playing with the parent club, his ice time was limited to various "spot duty" assignments, including several occasions when an "enforcer" was required. The team's other enforcer, Colton Orr, was injured mid-season after striking his head on the ice during a fight, so it was decided that Rosehill was needed on the club to carry out the "tough guy" role.

Fredrik Sjostrom is your typical journeyman hockey player. He performed well in a penalty-killing role. He is the kind of player that every team needs…a solid, dependable skater, possessed of a sound work ethic, and ready at all times to step into the line-up whenever he is needed. Versatile and dependable are adjectives appropriately applied to players like Freddie.

Darryl Boyce was called up to the parent club late in the season. He performed in a very impressive manner. He is a tough kid, as was shown when he sustained a very serious face injury, but donned a full facial mask in order to be ready to play in his very next game. Based upon the way he played, I would like to think that Darryl has considerable potential for next season as a full-time Leaf.

This year, the Maple Leafs were fortunate to have two very skilled left wingers in the persons of Nik Kulemin and Clarke MacArthur. Of the two, Kulemin possibly has the most pure, natural skills of a hockey player. He developed as a player in Russia, where he established a reputation for being a very skilled and highly dedicated player. He became a member of the thirty-goal club for the first time this season. In just 233 games in the NHL, Nik has garnered 61 goals and 63 assists. This set of relatively balanced statistics in an indicator that Kulemin places equal importance on setting goals up as well as hitting the back of the net himself. He definitely has the potential to become a superstar in the NHL.

Clarke MacArthur has had a stellar season for the Leafs this year. He began his NHL career with the Buffalo Sabres, then was traded to the Atlanta Thrashers, for whom he played last year. When the Thrashers declined to honour a $ 2.4 million salary arbitration awarded to MacArthur, he became a free agent. He was a former team-mate of Leaf Captain Dion Phaneuf when the two played together in the 2005 World Junior Championships, therefore he decided to sign a one-year deal with Toronto. He opened the campaign by scoring goals in the first four games, a feat unequalled by any Leaf player, past or present. He went on to become a consistent offensive threat for the Leafs all season long. I cannot help but think that he will be offered a contract extension by the Leafs before too much time passes this summer. Clarke is very personable, hard-working, and appears very dedicated to the future success of the Leaf franchise.

In summary then, the Leafs are in reasonably good shape on left wing. Kulemin, MacArthur, and Boyce are all young enough and skilled enough to pose a consistent offensive threat on the port side of the attack. Sjostrom and Rosehill have proven competent as blue-collar backup support staff. Hopefully, training camp in September will serve to refine and strengthen the effectiveness of these talented players.

Assessing the Right Wing

Finally, we come to the right side of the Maple Leaf attack. Here, we will examine the work of seven players who patrolled right wing on this team. Those young men were:

	GP	Goals	Assists	Points	+/	PIM
Phil Kessel (23)	82	32	32	64	-20	24
Joffrey Lupul (27)	28	9	9	18	-11	19
Colby Armstrong (28)	50	8	15	23	-1	38
Joey Crabb (28)	49	3	12	15	-1	
Mike Brown (25)	50	3	5	8	1	68
Colton Orr (29)	46	2	0	2	-1	128
Kris Versteeg (24)	*53*	*14*	*21*	*35*	*N/A*	*29*
Matt Frattin (23)	1	0	0	0	-1	0
TOTALS		**71**	**94**	**165**		

I will begin my evaluations of the Leaf right wingers by commenting upon Matt Frattin, who only appeared in a single game at the end of the schedule. Brian Burke recently signed him to a two-year Entry Level Contract. Frattin played for the University of North Dakota. He posted 60 points this season, and is a candidate for the Hobey Baker Award as best player in the NCAA Hockey League. It will be interesting to see how he develops within the Leaf organization.

I was very disappointed when Kris Versteeg was traded away from the Leafs at the end of February. He was a member of the Stanley Cup winning Chicago Blackhawks last season, and was well on his way to a solid, successful year in Toronto. Kris now toils for the Philadelphia Flyers, to whom he was traded for a couple of draft picks.

Colton Orr is the Leafs' main "enforcer". He will not get a lot of ice time in each game. He will not score many points. Nonetheless, he bears watching whenever he skates out for action, because there is, in all likelihood, an issue that needs to be addressed. Colton's season was cut short this year when he sustained a head injury that resulted in a concussion. He has a couple of years remaining on his Leaf contract.

Mike Brown, in my opinion, is another one of those hard-working, dedicated journeyman hockey players that are valued by every successful hockey team. Players like Mike are not renowned for putting up big numbers, but can always be depended upon when specific situations arise that suit their talents. Mike's contributions to this year's club were recently rewarded when he was offered a three-year contract extension. He will be proudly wearing the blue and white in many future Maple Leaf matches.

Leaf fans got a reasonably good look at Joey Crabb over the course of the 2010 – 2011 schedule, and for the most part I think that they liked what they saw. I view Joey in much the same light as his fellow winger, Mike Brown. He appears to be a solid, dependable player, ready to give his all in support of his team-mates. Joey is still very young, but should be nearing his optimum production years as a pro hockey player.

I felt really sorry for Colby Armstrong this season. Newly acquired from the Atlanta Thrashers, I got the sense that he genuinely wanted to be a major factor in the Leafs' resurgence to contender status. Sadly, though, Colby suffered not one, but TWO injuries that proved to be so serious that he missed a total of 32 games at two separate portions of the season. Colby is a very talented player, and he is certainly not one bit hesitant to get under the skin of his opponents. Colby has two more years remaining on his contract with the Leafs, and his positive, feisty approach to the game should bode well for Toronto's fortunes next year.

I believe that Joffrey Lupul has the potential to become a very important part of future success by the Toronto Maple Leafs. Joffrey was acquired by Brian Burke from the Anaheim Ducks. Toronto is Joffrey's fourth NHL team. In addition to the Ducks, Joffrey has also played for the Edmonton Oilers and the Philadelphia Flyers. Lupul's scoring statistics indicate that he is another player whose goal total (126) very closely matches his assists (130). I have mentioned elsewhere in this work that I admire players whose records seem to indicate that they don't really care whether they register a goal or an assist, as long as the puck winds up at the back of the opposition net. I sincerely hope that Joffrey's serious back problems are over, and that he can now look forward to his best years wearing the Maple Leaf jersey.

Much has been written about Phil Kessel this past season. Much will be written about Phil next year, too…and probably for many years to come. Phis Kessel is the cornerstone of Brian Burke's Maple Leafs. Acquiring Kessel from the Boston Bruins was one of the first items on Burke's agenda once he took the reins of the organization a bit more than two years ago. Years down the road, when Brian Burke's tenure in Toronto is over, his term as the General Manager of the Leafs will rise or fall on the success that the club attains with Kessel performing in a key role.

Let me make one thing perfectly clear, readers.

Phil Kessel is a star in the National Hockey League. This past season marked his third consecutive campaign in the "thirty goal club". (36, 30, 32) He has always been held in high regard in the world of hockey. **He is still a kid…only 23 years of age.**

Phil had a very successful season this year…make no mistake about that! Training camp went quite well for him. He played in 9 exhibition games, scoring 6 goals and 4 assists. His production numbers looked great as the new season approached.

Kessel didn't miss a single game all season long. He scored at least one point in 46 of the 82 games, posting totals of 32 goals and 32 assists…64 points in all. An examination of Phil's scoring record in the NHL reveals that he can be counted upon for .6 points per game…not quite superstar status…but close.

I believe that Phil Kessel is entirely capable of becoming a superstar in the NHL, and I sincerely hope that we will see him attain that status as a Maple Leaf.

Phil cannot become a superstar by himself. He needs help, and everyone who follows the Leafs knows that. Brian Burke's central responsibility during the summer of 2011 will be to get the centre that Phil needs to form a pre-eminent forward line for this team. If he is successful… or should I say **WHEN** he is successful, I believe that the Leafs can look forward to SEVERAL successful campaigns…**and maybe even a CUP or two!!!**

Phil Kessel is easy to read. When his level of play falls below the expectations that he sets for himself, you can tell by his facial expressions and his body language. He experienced several frustrations this year. The horrible collapse of the team in October and November frustrated him, along with all of his team-mates. It didn't help that he endured a scoring slump that stretched over several games. To cap all this off was the somewhat humiliating experience of being chosen LAST for his team at the All Star Game, although he WAS awarded a new car to help ease his agony.

I hope that Phil Kessel has a terrific year as the 2011 – 2012 season unfolds. He deserves it. He has overcome some very difficult challenges throughout his early years in the NHL…not the least of which was overcoming a bout of cancer. He knows what is expected of him in Toronto, and I wish him every success as he soldiers on with this team.

In conclusion, things look very good on right wing for next season's Maple Leafs. Six very sound players are already on staff, and there may even be two or three wannabes at training camp. Good luck to them.

How does one summarize or encapsulate exactly where things stand at the present time within the realm of the Toronto Maple Leafs? I offer the following:

<u>Management</u> **The jury is still out. Brian Burke has a good management team. However, the Leafs MUST make the playoffs next year, or else Burke's tenure in Toronto will be at grave risk.**

<u>Coaching</u> **The present coaching staff is inadequate. It is my position that a new Head Coach should be hired, and he should be enabled to assemble any assistants that he needs to fulfill his team's destiny.**

<u>Goaltending</u>	James Reimer is the main man. The backup position is wide open.
<u>Defence</u>	Captain Dion Phaneuf and the six other defenders currently in place <u>SHOULD</u> be capable of providing competent work on the blue line.
<u>Centre</u>	<u>**REMAINS A GLARING NEED.**</u> Burke should spare no expense to acquire a **BLUE RIBBON** centre for this team by way of either free agency or a trade. That player, plus the other centres on staff will strengthen this team adequately.
<u>Left Wing</u>	Not a problem area at present. Some very talented players are in place.
<u>Right Wing</u>	Another strong aspect of the team. As long as the present wingers can recover from injury and remain healthy next season, good things should happen.

And so, dear readers, this season's story ends. It has been another sad tale to tell, replete with a goodly portion of frustration for everyone in Leaf Nation.

But there is hope. The team is young. We could be witnessing the rebirth of the Heart and Spirit that I wrote about nine years ago, in a previous book.

The future is beginning to look bright. Will it be truth or illusion? Our answer lies in the future. We'll ALL have to: WAIT UNTIL NEXT YEAR.

Afterword # 1

Two Dark Clouds on the Current Season

Derek Boogaard played for the New York Rangers this past season. His role on the team was that of an "enforcer". On December 9, 2010, he was involved in a fight with Matt Carkner of the Ottawa Senators. In that fight, he sustained a concussion. It was so serious that he never played again for the rest of the season.

On May 13, just a few weeks ago, Derek was found dead in his apartment in Minneapolis, Minnesota. When I first heard of this tragedy, I was afraid that the worst fear of hockey fans everywhere had come to pass. A player in hockey's most elite league had died as the result of a concussion. With that possibility lurking in the background, Derek's parents agreed to donate his brain to Boston University Medical School, an organization deeply involved in the study of the effects of brain injuries suffered by athletes involved in several high-contact sports.

As it has turned out since Derek's tragic passing, there was another element that had a role in this event. As might be expected, Derek was using prescribed medications to aid in his recovery from the injury that he sustained. Sadly though, Derek, for whatever personal reasons he may have had, added alcohol into the situation. As has so often been the case, the combination of alcohol and medications proved to be lethal.

Could this horrible result have been prevented? How closely was Derek being supervised in his recovery? How frequently was he being seen, in person, by doctors charged with reporting to the New York Rangers hockey club? We may never find out the answers to all of these questions. Whatever the future brings, the death of Derek Boogaard, mere weeks before his 29th birthday, will remain a dark cloud over the 2010-2011 NHL season.

****

A second dark consequence that surfaces regularly in the sports news media has been the prolonged absence of Sidney Crosby from the game of hockey, which he has dominated for the past few years. Sid the Kid has not skated in the NHL since the first week in January. He, like Derek Boogaard, was unable to complete the regular season or participate in the playoffs because of a concussion.

It is now a matter of public record that 70 NHL players...fully 10 percent of those playing in the league, have missed playing time this season due to head injuries...most of them concussions. I consider this fact to be <u>ALARMING!</u>

It is my sincere hope that, over the course of this summer, both the NHL and the NHLPA work together to devise and implement every measure possible to reduce the catastrophic impact of head injuries on the game of hockey. The issue of concussions in professional sports cannot be minimized. Such issues have proven in many cases to be both career and life-altering.

As this is written, it has been reported that Sidney Crosby has been cleared by his doctors to resume an off-season training program to prepare for full participation in training camp in September. If all goes well between now and then, Sidney will be able to rejoin his Penguin team-mates, and hopefully resume his career as one of the greatest players to grace the sport. I wish the same good result for all of the players in the NHL who have had the misfortune to sustain head injuries this year.

****

To conclude this entry on a brighter note, I am delighted to report here that the National Hockey League has returned to Winnipeg, Manitoba. While it is unfortunate that the city of Atlanta, Georgia loses a major sports franchise, the reality was that the people there were simply not supporting that venture. Businesses that constantly lose millions of dollars must sooner or later face the consequences.

Atlanta's loss has become Winnipeg's gain. Canada now has SEVEN NHL clubs. In a short time, we will be informed of the official name of the Winnipeg team. Fifteen years ago, the club was known as the Jets. As of today, we just don't know whether or not that name will be resurrected, or a new one declared.

Canada, from coast to coast to coast, welcomes back the new Winnipeg hockey club. We deserve more, though, and it is my sincere hope that before too many more years pass, we will see two or more additional franchises in hockey's elite league. I definitely support the idea of a franchise in both Hamilton and Quebec City. I am also convinced that the tri-city area of Kitchener, Waterloo, and Cambridge could sustain an NHL franchise. As well, I view Halifax as a possibly NHL destination.

Hockey is Canada's game. It belongs here. Whenever and wherever it comes, I am sure that Canadians will support it and encourage its growth.

Afterword #2

The 2011 Stanley Cup Playoffs

Sixteen teams qualified for inclusion in this season's Stanley Cup Tournament. Here is a brief summary of the results, round by round

Eastern Quarter-Finals

Montreal vs. Boston

Game 1	**Montreal** 2	Boston 0	
Game 2	**Montreal** 3	Boston 1	
Game 3	Montreal 2	**Boston** 4	
Game 4	Montreal 4	**Boston** 5	**Boston Wins 4-3**
Game 5	Montreal 1	**Boston** 2	
Game 6	**Montreal** 2	Boston 1	
Game 7	Montreal 3	**Boston** 4	
TOTALS	17	17	

Washington vs. New York Rangers

Game 1	**Washington** 2	New York 1	
Game 2	**Washington** 2	New York 0	
Game 3	Washington 2	New York 3	**Washington Wins 4-1**
Game 4	**Washington** 4	New York 3	
Game 5	**Washington** 3	New York 1	
TOTALS	13	8	

Philadelphia vs. Buffalo

Game 1	Philadelphia 0	**Buffalo** 1	
Game 2	**Philadelphia** 5	Buffalo 4	
Game 3	**Philadelphia** 4	Buffalo 2	
Game 4	Philadelphia 0	**Buffalo** 1	**Washington Wins 4-3**
Game 5	Philadelphia 3	**Buffalo** 4	
Game 6	**Philadelphia** 5	Buffalo 4	
Game 7	**Philadelphia** 5	Buffalo 2	
TOTALS	22	18	

Pittsburgh vs. Tampa Bay

Game 1	**Pittsburgh 3**	Tampa Bay 0	
Game 2	Pittsburgh 1	**Tampa Bay 5**	
Game 3	**Pittsburgh 3**	Tampa Bay 2	
Game 4	**Pittsburgh 3**	**Tampa Bay 2**	**Tampa Bay Wins 4-3**
Game 5	Pittsburgh 2	**Tampa Bay 8**	
Game 6	Pittsburgh 2	**Tampa Bay 4**	
Game 7	Pittsburgh 0	**Tampa Bay 1**	
TOTALS	14	22	

Western Quarter Finals

Vancouver vs. Chicago

Game 1	**Vancouver 2**	Chicago 0	
Game 2	**Vancouver 4**	Chicago 3	
Game 3	**Vancouver 3**	Chicago 2	
Game 4	Vancouver 2	**Chicago 7**	**Vancouver Wins 4-3**
Game 5	Vancouver 0	**Chicago 5**	
Game 6	Vancouver 3	**Chicago 4**	
Game 7	**Vancouver 2**	Chicago 1	
TOTALS	16	22	

San Jose vs. Los Angeles

Game 1	**San Jose 3**	Los Angeles 2	
Game 2	San Jose 0	**Los Angeles 4**	
Game 3	**San Jose 6**	Los Angeles 5	
Game 4	**San Jose 6**	Los Angeles 3	**San Jose Wins 4-2**
Game 5	San Jose 1	**Los Angeles 3**	
Game 6	**San Jose 4**	Los Angeles 3	
TOTALS	20	20	

Detroit vs. Phoenix

Game 1	**Detroit 4**	Phoenix 2	
Game 2	**Detroit 4**	Phoenix 3	
Game 3	**Detroit 4**	Phoenix 2	**Detroit Wins 4-0**
Game 4	**Detroit 6**	Phoenix 3	
TOTALS	18	10	

Anaheim vs. Nashville

Game 1	Anaheim 1	**Nashville 4**	
Game 2	**Anaheim 5**	Nashville 3	
Game 3	Anaheim 3	**Nashville 4**	**Naashville Wins 4-2**
Game 4	**Anaheim 6**	Nashville 3	
Game 5	Anaheim 3	**Nashville 4**	
Game 6	Anaheim 2	**Nashville 4**	
TOTALS	20	22	

Eastern Semi-Finals

Philadelphia vs. Boston

Game 1	Philadelphia 3	**Boston 7**	
Game 2	Philadelphia 2	**Boston 3**	
Game 3	Philadelphia 1	**Boston 5**	**Boston Wins 4-0**
Game 4	Philadelphia 1	**Boston 5**	
TOTALS	7	20	

Washington vs. Tampa Bay

Game 1	Washington 2	**Tampa Bay 4**	
Game 2	Washington 2	**Tampa Bay 3**	
Game 3	Washington 3	**Tampa Bay 4**	**Tampa Bay Wins 4-0**
Game 4	Washington 3	**Tampa Bay 5**	
TOTALS	10	16	

Western Semi-Finals

Vancouver vs. Nashville

Game 1	**Vancouver 1**	Nashville 0	
Game 2	Vancouver 1	**Nashville 2**	
Game 3	**Vancouver 3**	Nashville 2	
Game 4	**Vancouver 4**	Nashville 2	**Vancouver Wins 4-2**
Game 5	Vancouver 3	**Nashville 4**	
Game 6	**Vancouver 2**	Nashville 1	
TOTALS	14	11	

San Jose vs. Detroit

Game 1	**San Jose 2**	Detroit 1	
Game 2	**San Jose 2**	Detroit 1	
Game 3	**San Jose 4**	Detroit 3	
Game 4	San Jose 3	**Detroit 4**	**San Jose Wins 4-3**
Game 5	San Jose 3	**Detroit 4**	
Game 6	San Jose 1	**Detroit 3**	
Game 7	**San Jose 3**	Detroit 2	
TOTALS	18	18	

Eastern Conference Final

Tampa Bay vs. Boston

Game 1	**Tampa Bay 5**	Boston 2	
Game 2	Tampa Bay 5	**Boston 6**	
Game 3	Tampa Bay 0	**Boston 2**	
Game 4	**Tampa Bay 5**	Boston 3	**Boston Wins 4-3**
Game 5	Tampa Bay 1	**Boston 3**	
Game 6	**Tampa Bay 5**	Boston 4	
Game 7	Tampa Bay 0	**Boston 1**	
TOTALS	21	21	

Western Conference Final

Vancouver vs. San Jose

Game 1	**Vancouver 3**	San Jose 2	
Game 2	**Vancouver 7**	San Jose 3	
Game 3	Vancouver 3	**San Jose 4**	**Vancouver Wins 4-1**
Game 4	**Vancouver 4**	San Jose 2	
Game 5	**Vancouver 3**	San Jose 2	
TOTALS	20	13	

The Stanley Cup Final

Vancouver Canucks vs. Boston Bruins

Game 1	**Vancouver** 1	Boston	0
Game 2	**Vancouver** 3	Boston	2
Game 3	Vancouver 1	**Boston**	8
Game 4	Vancouver 0	**Boston**	4
Game 5	**Vancouver** 1	Boston	0
Game 6	Vancouver 2	**Boston**	5
Game 7	Vancouver 0	**Boston**	4
TOTALS	8		23

The Boston Bruins are Stanley Cup Champions.

Bruin goalie Tim Thomas won the Conn Smythe Trophy, awarded to the most outstanding player in the Stanley Cup playoffs.

Following Game 7, there was a massive riot in the streets of Downtown Vancouver, perpetrated by a bunch of drunken morons who know little and care less about the great game of hockey.

Some Final Observations

The following is a list of the teams were the best performers in the NHL this season. Along with their names, I have listed their regular season point totals and their ultimate fate in the playoffs.

<u>Team</u>	<u>Regular Season Points</u>	<u>Playoff Fate</u>
Vancouver Canucks	117	Lost in Finals
Washington Capitals	107	Lost ¼ Final
Philadelphia Flyers	106	Lost ¼ Final
Pittsburgh Penguins	106	Lost in Round 1
San Jose Sharks	105	Lost Semi-Final
Detroit Red Wings	104	Lost ¼ Final
Tampa Bay Lightning	103	Lost Semi-Final
Boston Bruins	**103**	**Won Stanley Cup**

Both teams that played off in the final series for the Stanley Cup played a total of 107 games this season…82 in the regular season and 25 in the playoffs.

Boston outscored Vancouver in the playoffs by a wide margin…81 goals to Vancouver's 58.

<u>Vancouver's scoring simply "dried up" in the playoffs. They scored only 8 goals in the final series for the Cup.</u>

<u>Roberto Luongo played very poorly on the road in the final series.</u> Those fickle "gods of hockey" conspired openly against the Canucks in the final game, and they were impotent in mounting any kind of attack against the victorious Bruins.

Congratulations to the Boston Bruins!

The Bruins proved to be the best team in 2010 – 2011. They truly deserve the title of <u>Stanley Cup Champions!</u>

About the Author

The author has been an avid follower of the Toronto Maple Leaf hockey club for almost six decades. Nine years ago, he wrote and published his first book, Entitled "Heart and Spirit: The Toronto Maple Leafs of 2001-2002" it was popular reading for Maple Leaf fans internationally.